PIRATES

OF THE

Chesapeake Bay

From the Colonial Era to the Oyster Wars

JAMIE L.H. GOODALL

THE
History
PRESS

Published by The History Press
Charleston, SC
www.historypress.com

For Kyle

CONTENTS

CONTENTS

TIMELINE OF MAJOR CONFLICTS

(1635–1659)	Franco-Spanish War
(1639–1651)	Wars of the Three Kingdoms
(1642–1651)	English Civil War
(1652–1654)	First Anglo-Dutch War
(1654–1660)	Anglo-Spanish War
(1665–1667)	Second Anglo-Dutch War
(1672–1678)	Franco-Dutch War
(1672–1674)	Third Anglo-Dutch War
(1688–1689)	Glorious Revolution
(1688–1697)	Nine Years' War
(1701–1714)	War of Spanish Succession
(1727–1729)	Anglo-Spanish War
(1754–1763)	French and Indian War or Seven Years' War
(1775–1783)	American Revolution
(1778–1783)	Anglo-French War
(1779–1783)	Anglo-Spanish War
(1780–1784)	Fourth Anglo-Dutch War
(1798–1800)	Quasi War
(1801–1805)	First Barbary War
(1803–1815)	Napoleonic Wars
(1812–1815)	War of 1812
(1815)	Second Barbary War
(1861–1865)	American Civil War
(1865–1959)	Chesapeake Oyster Wars

ACKNOWLEDGEMENTS

*F*irst, I'd like to thank my editor, Kate Jenkins, and the team at Arcadia Publishing and The History Press for picking this project up. Kate's constant support and the team's utmost professionalism and expertise made writing this book a wonderful experience. I would also like to thank Stevenson University, the university's library staff and Diane Payne with the Office of Sponsored Programs and Research (OSPR) for their financial and professional support in this endeavor. This project would have been much more difficult to complete without the assistance of the OSPR's writing retreats.

I'd also like to extend my gratitude to my dearest colleagues, Dr. Amanda Licastro and Dr. Kerry Spencer. Their tireless faith in me, their uplifting messages when I felt like I couldn't power through and their generous offers to read any and everything I had written were critical in the completion of this book. As was the feedback I received on the framework of the book from Herb Childress. I also sincerely appreciate the focused writing time and support of my writing group colleagues Amanda, Kerry, Mauyaugust Finkenburg and Aaron Chandler.

I would also like to say thank you to the Library of Congress and the Metropolitan Museum of Art for their outstanding open access work that made the inclusion of the beautiful images within these pages possible. A debt of gratitude is also owed to the scholars whose fantastic work on the various aspects of the Chesapeake aided me in my research efforts. I want to extend special thanks to my department chair, Glenn Johnston, for setting me up with an important newspaper repository when I thought all hope was lost and to my research assistants Mina Altman and Jessica Miller for their endeavors in easing some of my own research burdens.

Lastly, and perhaps most importantly, a simple thank-you cannot express the gratitude I hold for my husband, Kyle. He was the cheerleader in my corner and did whatever he could with his hectic schedule to ensure that I had everything I needed every time I sat down to write. Without him and our precious pups, Thomas Jefferson and John Tyler, I wouldn't be where I am today.

INTRODUCTION

orn to a family of middling means in Kent, William Claiborne wanted a life and legacy grander than those of his predecessors. Although his father and grandfather seized odd investment opportunities in shipping and small industrial enterprises, neither ever exceeded the position of local alderman and lord mayor in King's Lynn, Norfolk. So, when he was offered the chance to leave King's Lynn and venture to Virginia as a land surveyor in 1621, Claiborne took it without hesitation. As a colonial official in Virginia, Claiborne wasted no time in taking advantage of his lucrative position. His office granted an annual salary of £30 (plus fees) and an immediate land grant of two hundred acres. In the first few years, Claiborne managed to secure three additional land grants from the colony's council, totaling nine hundred acres, and his salary was doubled on a retroactive basis. Eventually, Claiborne was able to work his way from surveyor to councilor and ultimately became the colony's secretary of state.[1]

Despite Claiborne's success, his ambitions weren't satisfied. In April 1627, Claiborne was granted a commission from Sir George Yeardley, governor and captain general of Virginia, which granted him full authority to discover the "remaining divers [sic] places and parts of this kingdom of Virginia altogether unknown." Claiborne was tasked with sailing "into any [of] the rivers, creeks, ports and havens within the Bay of Chesapeake" and establishing trade relations with local indigenous populations, particularly those in the fur trade.[2] Between March 1629 and May 1631, Claiborne was granted three additional commissions of a similar scope, setting physical

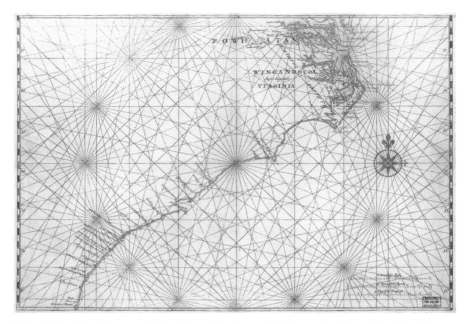

Map of the Atlantic coast of North America, from the Chesapeake Bay to Florida, 1639.
Courtesy of the Library of Congress Geography and Map Division.

parameters "within the degrees of thirty-four and forty-one."[3] Claiborne chose to center his operations on Kent Island with the goal of provisioning and trading along the coast between Virginia and Nova Scotia, easily securing funding from London merchants like William Cloberry.

What should have been a simple and profitable scheme was anything but. While seeking funding in London, Claiborne learned that George Calvert, First Baron Baltimore, was using his influence to stake out a Catholic colony just north of Virginia. Claiborne kept to his plan, bringing one hundred men to Kent Island and building, planting and settling for the entirety of 1631 until the island was officially represented in the Virginia Assembly. Yet Calvert prevailed in his own venture. Although George Calvert died in April 1632, he had convinced King Charles I to grant the Calvert family a charter to settle "thirty-eight to forty degrees of land unplanted." Ownership of the property was assumed by Calvert's son Cecilius, Second Lord Baltimore, later that summer. To Claiborne's dismay, this new charter technically placed Kent Island—land and cattle that was valued over £7,000—under the control of Maryland and the Calvert family.[4] A series of territorial debates and maritime conflicts ensued, with Claiborne at the helm.

In 1635, an agent of Claiborne's named Thomas Smith seized a pinnace near Palmer's Island as it headed to the colony of Maryland.[5] Smith carried the pinnace, which contained a "great quantitie [*sic*] of trucking commodities," and its commanders to Kent Island. While there, John Butler—Claiborne's brother-in-law—confiscated the goods and imprisoned its commanders. To Calvert, Claiborne's actions constituted a clear act of piracy. Although Claiborne ordered the release of the men quite quickly, he wasn't done disrupting the new colony's trade. A short time later, Claiborne again sent the pinnace *Long Tayle*—under the captaincy of Thomas Smith—to Mattapany Village to establish trade with the indigenous population. However, there was one small problem: the village was within the boundaries of St. Mary's, Maryland. Upon Smith's arrival to the area, Calvert's ship captains stopped him and demanded proof of his right to trade in the area. When Smith produced copies of the king's commission that had been granted to Claiborne, Calvert's captains determined that the document had been falsified and was based on false information. They seized the *Long Tayle*, arrested Smith and brought him and his men to Maryland. After several days, Governor Calvert released the men but kept the *Long Tayle* and its cargo—which was primarily cloth and beaver skins—leaving the men to make their own way home.[6] To Claiborne, *this* was the real act of piracy, and he vowed to seek revenge for his losses.

Claiborne placed Lieutenant Ratcliffe Warren in charge of a newly armed sloop called the *Cockatrice*. Warren was under express orders to "make reprisals" on any vessel belonging to a Maryland resident, but Governor Calvert anticipated Claiborne's next move and sent, not one, but two armed vessels to deal with this next depredation: the *St. Margaret* (under the command of Cuthbert Fenwick) and the *St. Helen* (led by Captain Thomas Cornwalleys). Outnumbered, Warren's men were forced to surrender after Warren and two of his men were killed. The Marylanders only lost one of their own men. Two more fights broke out at the end of May, including Smith's exacting victory over Cornwalleys. Claiborne took advantage of the momentum and sent Captain Philip Taylor to recapture the *Long Tayle*, but the plan failed, and Taylor was taken prisoner.

Battles—both physical and legal—continued intermittently over the next few years. In 1637, Thomas Smith, John Butler and his associate Edward Beckler were arrested and detained on accusations of "sedition, pyracie and murther" in Maryland. Additionally, a grand inquest was held at St. Mary's to determine Claiborne's role when the *Cockatrice* "feloniously" attacked the *St. Helen* and *St. Margaret* "as pyrates and robbers." In March 1638, Claiborne

Home of William Claiborne, Sweet Hall, in King William County, Virginia, built circa 1700. Photograph taken in 1935. *Courtesy of the Library of Congress Carnegie Survey of the Architecture of the South.*

was officially charged with piracy. Although Claiborne was spared the same fate as Smith and Beckler—who were both hanged for piracy in June 1638— he lost his goods, lands, tenements and cattle, and his former reputation as an important Virginia official was destroyed.[7]

Although the actions of Claiborne and his associates marked the first recorded convictions (and executions) of piracy in the Chesapeake, they were not the last. In many ways, Claiborne's path to piracy mirrors the experiences of hundreds of men who were engaged in the illicit economy of the early modern Atlantic world. Some of them were bored merchants in the midst of a midlife crisis, like Stede Bonnet, who sold his business, ditched his wife and paid for a pirate crew. Others were pirate-hunters-turned-pirate, like William Kidd. However, most were average men: sailors, merchants, fathers and sons. Their piratical adventures were mostly short lived; they drank in taverns, invested in businesses, bought homes and most even settled down with wives and families. Some pirates were from the Chesapeake, while others just attacked the region. Some used the Chesapeake as a marketplace for stolen goods, while others sought to defend the region as privateers. The history of piracy in the Chesapeake is a story of relationships and opportunism, adventure and bloodshed, economics and politics. Every good story has four key elements: characters (Who were the people involved in acts of piracy and what was their role?), setting (Where were the depredations occurring and with what locations in the Chesapeake did piracy become inextricably linked?), conflict (Why the Chesapeake? What made this particular region a haven for or prime target of pirates?) and resolution (What brought it all to an end?).

THE CHARACTERS

Pirates and Privateers

From the Elizabethan Sea Dogs to the so-called golden age of piracy, commerce raiders maintained a prominent place in people's imaginations. Depending on who you were and which side of a conflict you were on, pirates were called many things: corsairs, buccaneers, privateers or even rebels. Pirates mainly operated on the open seas, but they were also known to make use of rivers and land to support their operations. The bulk of piratical depredations occurred during the golden age of piracy, a period that spanned from the 1650s to the 1730s. Pirates in the Chesapeake were part of a much larger phenomenon that many referred to as a brotherhood, or the Brethren of the Coast. The brotherhood was a very loose coalition of pirates (and privateers) with bases in Tortuga, Nassau and Port Royal. They promoted the idea of a "pirate's code," or a set of agreements regarding everything from the division of loot to the appointment of a captain. As a result of this code, some scholars, like Marcus Rediker, argue that pirate ships were seaborne egalitarian communities. The men on them shared equal votes in terms of where to sail and who to attack, and they had an equitable division of plunder and labor. But not all pirates considered themselves a part of this brotherhood, and there was not always honor among thieves. While these men may not have stolen from someone on their own ship, there wasn't much stopping them from stealing from another pirate ship. Sometimes, these men even took whole ships, like when Captain Culliford stole Captain Kidd's ship or when Walter Kennedy stole a ship from Black Bart Roberts.

Most pirates didn't start out as pirates; merchant marines and sailors with the Royal Navy frequently turned to piracy when given the chance. After becoming fed up with constant, brutal beatings and lack of pay, the sailors would mutiny against their officers. If a ship was boarded by a pirate crew, sailors would sometimes opt to join the rogues rather than remain in their ship's employment. If caught and tried for piracy, many of these men would claim that they had been "forced" to join.

Technically, there were only two things that separated a privateer from a pirate: perspective and a letter of marque. Both pirates and privateers had one main job: attack and plunder ships, but in times of conflict, government officials permitted people to arm their personal vessels and attack enemy ships in order to disrupt trade. In essence, a letter of marque merely gave the act of piracy the façade of legitimacy. While privateering was often viewed as an honorable and patriotic duty (augmenting naval forces), piracy was widely considered a scourge on the seas. In reality, the lines were not sharply defined, and privateers often strayed from their intended path. Privateers were little more than legally sanctioned pirates whose actions were clearly piratical under the rule of law but purposefully went unpunished.[8] In a letter of marque, the name of the enemy nation (or nations) was clearly stated and all prizes were to be brought before an Admiralty Court to determine its status. There were supposed to be heavy penalties if a privateer seized the ship of a neutral nation, but many privateers felt it better to ask for forgiveness rather than permission. Once the prizes were deemed legitimate, neutral nations often made complaints to the offending governments for their losses. They also sometimes tried these so-called privateers as pirates after refusing to recognize their letter of marque as legitimate. In some of these cases, the privateers would even be executed before anything could be done. Reverend Cotton Mather once lamented that privateering "easily degenerates into the piratical…and proves an inlet unto so much debauchery, and iniquity, and confusion." He hoped all good Christian men would support him in its opposition.[9]

So, why would a privateer risk an attack on a neutral ship? The first—and most obvious—reason is greed. The captain and crew of a privateering vessel were not paid a salary, and the owner of the vessel would only make a return on his investment if the venture was successful. Any money that privateers received came from the sale of the captured ship and its cargo. Part of the profits went to the privateers, another part went to the vessel's owner and another went to the Crown.[10] So, if a privateer wanted to get paid and there were no enemy ships around, they may have had to settle for a neutral one.

The second reason a privateer may have attacked a neutral ship is that the news of a peace agreement between nations may not have reached them in time. In this case, they would seize a vessel believing it to still be an enemy prize. The third possible reason for a privateer's attack on a neutral ship is the fact that, between the seventeenth and eighteenth centuries, European nations found themselves entangled in no fewer than a dozen conflicts, and allegiances during—and between—these conflicts frequently shifted. So, an attack on a neutral vessel may merely have been done out of confusion.

What about the neutral goods that were being carried by belligerent vessels? The blurred line between piracy and privateering continued to cause confusion and economic losses well into the nineteenth century. Tired of the failed attempts at regulating privateering, fifty-five nations (including France and Britain) signed the Paris Declaration Respecting Maritime Law in 1856. The United States did not sign the declaration, as the nation was concerned about the lack of a strong navy. Not signing allowed the United States to use privateers during the American Civil War and the Spanish-American War.

Smugglers

Smuggling is defined by *Merriam-Webster* as "to import or export secretly, contrary to the law and especially without paying duties imposed by law" or "to convey or introduce surreptitiously." Some, like historian Alan Karras, argue that piracy and smuggling are two words that "connote altogether different sorts of legal transgressions."[11] If we operate purely based on definition, that might be true, as *Merriam-Webster* defines piracy as "an act of robbery on the high seas…specifically an illegal act of violence, detention or plunder committed for private ends by [the] crew or passengers of a private ship or aircraft against another ship or aircraft on the high seas or in a place outside the jurisdiction of any state." However, if we move beyond the simplistic definitions of these two actions, we can better see how pirates often acted as smugglers when the act of robbing on the open waters was complete. How else would they have sold their ill-gotten goods in legitimate marketplaces? While Karras might argue that the customers of goods brought in by smugglers looked just like any other consumer, how is that different from pirates? So, while I refer primarily to the actions in this book as piracy, I will use smuggling where it is appropriate. Both pirates and smugglers were affected by the English Navigation Acts that were passed at the beginning of 1651. Chesapeake residents looked to pirates, merchants and local government officials to bypass these trading obstacles in order to meet their demands for affordable manufactured goods from Europe and the Caribbean.

Merchants, Government Officials and Local Residents

The titles of merchant, government official and local resident easily overlapped in the Chesapeake Bay. On one hand, all three groups provided considerable aid to pirates, and on the other hand, these groups could be legal thorns in their sides. Both merchants and government officials were— by their very duty and nature—considered local residents. Merchants often served as government officials, and merchants and local residents could become pirates. The relationships between these different groups wove a complex web. This book uses the phrase "government official" to encompass a variety of positions and changing titles. "Government official" might refer to a monarch, a president, a governor, an admiralty judge, a secretary of state or a councilor. This book uses "merchant" to refer to retailers, wholesalers and shopkeepers for the sake of simplicity. This book primarily uses "local residents" to refer to those who inhabited the broader Chesapeake (Maryland and Virginia) region. But, where relevant, this book will use more specific and appropriate titles.

THE SETTING

So, where did the majority of these acts of piracy and privateering occur and what locations became inextricably linked with the pirates and privateers from the region? The Chesapeake Bay region encompasses both Maryland and Virginia, and the bay extends for two hundred miles from Havre de Grace, Maryland, to Virginia Beach, Virginia. Piracy affected a number of locations—big and small—in the Chesapeake Bay region. When looking at Maryland, specifically, acts of piracy occurred in places like Palmer's Island, Annapolis, Baltimore, St. Mary's City, the Eastern Shore and Fell's Point, just to name a few. When looking at Virginia, this book will particularly look at Richmond, Williamsburg, Blackbeard's Point and Chincoteague.

Ship at Sea, watercolor, late nineteenth century by Albert Ernest Markes. *Courtesy of the Metropolitan Museum of Art.*

THE CONFLICT

Why did pirates choose the Chesapeake? The economy of the Chesapeake was based on the region's accessibility, which made it a convenient spot for importing and exporting goods and people across the Atlantic. The region's access to fresh water and fertile soil also made it agriculturally productive; in particular, the English found that tobacco grew easily in the Chesapeake region. The Chesapeake region's production of tobacco boomed after John Rolfe brought a sweeter strain of seeds to Virginia from his voyage to Tobago in 1612. Large-scale tobacco plantations began popping up along the rivers and shorelines of Virginia and Maryland through the late 1600s and early 1700s. For example, on the lower Western Shore of Maryland, there was a small group of gentry-held plantations that ranged in sizes from 100 acres to 5,400 acres; on average, however, these individual plantations comprised about 1,000 acres of land.[12] With the exception of a brief lull in profitability between 1680 and 1700, this profitable product led to the passage of a series of "Tobacco Acts" by the colonial governments of the Chesapeake. These acts regulated everything, from inspecting the hogsheads of tobacco that were intended for sale or use as currency, to standardizing tobacco by grading it. A system known as the Chesapeake Consignment System gave rise to Tobacco Lords and a cycle of "leaf demand, slave labor demand and global commerce." Tobacco placed the Chesapeake squarely in a relationship with merchants and wholesalers in London, Charleston and New Orleans.[13]

By the mid-eighteenth century, tobacco accounted for roughly 72 percent of exports by value in the Chesapeake and 29 percent in the whole of the colonies. As the British attempted to assert their control over the region, Chesapeake residents and merchants began throwing their support behind subversive movements, such as piracy, smuggling and even the push for independence. Additionally, regulations and high demand not only increased the profits from tobacco, but they also required a significant growth of the region's labor force of enslaved Africans. Pirates were all too happy to provide that labor and steal that tobacco for their own profit. The society of the Chesapeake was not marked by the same extremes of wealth and poverty as other regions in the Atlantic. At the top, they maintained a small but moderately wealthy merchant class, in the middle was a rather large group of small and middling planters and at the bottom was a "great mass" of indentured servants.[14]

War helped increase the presence of pirates in the Chesapeake region. The War of the League of Augsburg (1689–1697) and the War of Spanish Succession (1701–1713) widely disrupted transatlantic trade, including Chesapeake exports of tobacco to London. A stagnation in the Chesapeake's economy meant that pirates afforded local residents, merchants and government officials the ability to import the European goods that they were previously unable to afford or acquire during war. This was a pattern that continued into the seventeenth and eighteenth centuries, during periods of incessant warfare.

As for the role of privateers, internal and external conflicts spawned the need for them in the absence of an American naval force. In particular, the importance of privateers to the American cause can be seen in three key conflicts: the American Revolution, the War of 1812 and the American Civil War. During the American Revolution, private vessels were utilized to stave off as many British incursions as possible; and more often than not, they were used to obstruct Britain's trade. Despite the peace that existed between the United States and Britain in 1783, the British began kidnapping American sailors and forcing them to serve in the Royal Navy in the early nineteenth century. At the time, Britain was at war with France, and they were trying to prevent Americans from trading with them. As a result of this practice—known as impressment—another war broke out: the War of 1812. This time, the war was between the British and the Americans. During the American Civil War, the Confederate States of America (CSA) resorted to the use of privateers as a defense against the U.S. Navy under the command of the Union. The CSA hoped their presence would prevent the formation of a blockade around Southern ports. The privateers served a secondary purpose: they attacked shipping vessels that were coming into and leaving the United States as a means of collecting a profit from the cargo and obtaining new ships.

After the American Civil War, the oyster harvesting industry in the Chesapeake region skyrocketed. As a response, Maryland formed the Maryland Oyster Navy in 1868 (a precursor to the Maryland Natural Resources police). A series of conflicts between oyster pirates, legal watermen and the Oyster Navy erupted and became collectively known as the Oyster Wars. Although these conflicts lasted until 1959, this book will focus primarily on those conflicts between 1865 and 1890. What follows is a collection of stories that follow some of the Chesapeake's most notorious pirates and valiant privateers and the local residents, merchants and government officials who aided, abetted and sometimes captured them. Batten down the hatches—we're about to head between the Devil and the deep blue sea.

PART I

THE COLONIES, THE CROWN AND THE PIRATES

1630–1750

*T*he Chesapeake colonies were developed as a means to an economic end: money, money and more money. The first Virginians arrived in the region in 1607; the first enslaved Africans were forcibly brought to the Chesapeake region in 1619; and in 1634, the first English colonists were sent to settle Maryland. Both Virginia and Maryland became key tobacco-producing colonies, and they reaped the profits of this industry off the backs of enslaved black laborers. But what role did pirates play in developing the economy and society of the Chesapeake? We know that William Claiborne's piracy was born of conflict between the inhabitants of Virginia and the settlers of Maryland over territory and resources. The Chesapeake also saw a Frenchman, a tobacco trader and a shipwreck salvager turn to piracy; numerous sailors and privateers hung up their legal hats for a life of illicit commerce. These men were integral parts of the Chesapeake's broader development.

RICHARD INGLE

Throughout the 1630s and early 1640s, Richard Ingle made it his business to transport goods and people across the Atlantic. Ingle primarily made his money in the tobacco trade and by all accounts did not start his career as a pirate. In 1641, he even ferried Thomas Cornwalleys and Leonard Calvert, the governor of Maryland, to St. Mary's after a brief trip to England. Cornwalleys proved to be a good friend and business associate of Ingle. When the English Civil War erupted the following year, the fates of Ingle, Calvert and Cornwalleys became even more interwoven.

The war was ultimately a conflict between the Roundheads of Parliament and the Royalists who were loyal to King Charles I. Although King Charles I was an Anglican, his marriage to the Catholic French princess Henrietta Maria led many to believe that he held private Catholic sympathies. He had also been the one to grant the Calvert family their colonial charter. Governor Calvert feared what would happen to the colony of Maryland, a haven for Catholics, should Parliament win the war. Would they revoke the charter in favor of someone who supported Parliament? When the war broke out, the American colonies tried to remain neutral, but after finding it difficult to maintain a neutral status, the colonies became divided. The Chesapeake colonies remained loyal to the king and did their part to support him. After they received orders to seize ships and goods belonging to Parliament and their "traitorous companies," Giles Brent (the acting governor in Calvert's absence) immediately set about fulfilling them.[15]

Richard Ingle, on the other hand, was raised as a Protestant and found himself in favor of Parliament's rejection of King Charles I's absolutist rule. The first accusations levied against Ingle were done so in an act of revenge in 1643 and 1644. A man named William Hardige was angry with Ingle for taking him to court over tobacco debts—not that it was the first time Hardige had been sued over debt he'd incurred—and since he knew of Ingle's Protestant background, Hardige accused him of high treason against King Charles I. Additionally, Hardige was summoned to give evidence against Ingle for "pyratical and treasonable offences" in the Chesapeake area. Ingle was unwittingly arrested, held without bond and had his goods and ship, the *Reformation*, seized. The sheriff, Edward Parker, was ordered to keep watch over Ingle. This was no easy task, since there was apparently no prison to hold him in. Parker was told that under no circumstances was Ingle to re-board his ship without express permission—in writing—from the acting governor.[16] But Ingle would not be prisoner long.

Ingle's escape was nothing short of brazen. It's unclear whether bribery was involved, but Cornwalleys and two other councilmen came to Parker and claimed they had license to take Ingle. Parker let Ingle go under the pretense that the acting governor had issued an order for his release since three prominent officials came to retrieve him. However, he reported that he went with the men to continue his watch over Ingle. All four men took Ingle to his ship, which he boarded. Cornwalleys then ordered Parker and his men to lay down their arms and get lost. According to Parker, they really had no choice but to run since several of Ingle's men came aboard and "beat and wounded some of the guards." Multiple juries were convened in an attempt to arrest and convict Ingle; however, each jury came back with "insufficient evidence" to prosecute.[17]

Brent made one final attempt to seize Ingle; he issued a warrant for his arrest on the grounds that he had assaulted the "vessels, guns, goods and person" of a man named Bishop. When threatened with arrest, Ingle reportedly said he would destroy the homes of local residents, including that of Brent. He was officially charged with "pyracie, mutinie, trespasse, contempt and misdemeanors." If Ingle hadn't been a pirate before, he was certainly at that point.[18] Ingle wasn't Calvert's only concern; the intrepid William Claiborne was back, taking advantage of the political turmoil of the time to recapture Kent Island. So, Calvert had a two-front conflict against "pirates and rogues."

First, Ingle and his men arrived with several other armed vessels and sacked St. Mary's. They held many members of the council prisoner, forced the governor into exile in Virginia and seized the estates of many Royalists, banishing them from the province.[19] Shortly after taking control of St. Mary's, Ingle moved on to St. Inigoes Creek, which just so happened to be in the same area as Cornwalleys's home. It seemed that Ingle and his crew were rather indiscriminate in their devastations. Cornwalleys was in England at the time, and his lawyer, Fenwick, was overseeing the property, so Ingle made his move. He convinced several servants to ignore Fenwick's request to retrieve his pinnace full of clothing, bedding and other goods that were valued at £250. This gave Ingle the opportunity to plunder the vessel while he sent his associates to sack and pillage the nearby homes. In the meantime, several of Ingle's men terrorized and held Cornwalleys's servants and Fenwick hostage.

Ingle himself got Fenwick rip-roaring drunk in the hopes of plundering Cornwalleys's home "legally." He convinced Fenwick that if he would just sign a note to his wife, the acting mistress of the house, permitting Ingle's men to seize Cornwalleys's home, arsenal and pinnace, then Ingle would let him go and promised that no harm would come to him. Worried for his own skin, Fenwick did as he was requested. But as soon as Fenwick delivered the note, Ingle ordered his men to seize him once again, and another group of men occupied Cornwalleys's home. The home was described as being full of furnishings, linen, bedding, pewter, brass and "all manner of household stuff" worth over £1,000. Cornwalleys was also one of the richest men in Maryland, so his home was filled with fineries, including Turkish carpets, East Indian spices, "satin damask petticoats laced with gold and silver" and a large cypress chest that was valued at £130 on its own. Ingle's men were accused of killing all the swine, goats and cattle and taking a "great store of beer, wine and 'strong waters.'"[20] According to Cornwalleys, not only did Ingle steal £200 worth of tobacco from him, but the value of goods seized from his property was more than £2,500. Ingle's men also allegedly took four enslaved black people and twelve men and maidservants.[21]

Ingle, however, told a different story. In a petition to Parliament in 1645, he reminded them of a letter of marque they issued to him and his ship, the *Reformation*, the previous year. This letter granted him the authority to seize the goods and ships of any Royalist vessel, which technically made him a privateer. Additionally, he believed he was acting based on the oath he made to aid and assist any Protestants who were affected by "tyranicall" rule. When he voyaged back to Maryland in 1643, he found a government under "tyrannical rule." The government of Maryland had been granted commissions from the Crown to seize goods and vessels belonging to Parliament and their supporters. He claimed that he saw his fellow Protestants being oppressed and threatened by a "tyrannicall governor and the Papists and malignants his adherents" and that he risked his life and fortune to assist them. Ingle went so far as to say that it "pleased God to enable him" to take from the "papists" their worldly possessions. He also said that these "papists" were conspiring against him with fictitious accounts of treason and piracy. Ingle encouraged Parliament to take action, as he believed that it would set a dangerous precedent to allow these people to make such false allegations against those fighting on behalf of Parliament.[22]

Regardless of whose version you believe, nearly two years of piracy and hardship befell Catholic Maryland in a period that later became known as the Plundering Time. There was no settled government to put a stop to piratical incursions, so Ingle wasn't done quite yet. He made good on his promise to pillage the property of Giles Brent on Kent Island and took his pinnace, the *Shotlocker*, that was filled with guns, linens, clothes and account books valued at £200. Ingle also seized a pinnace called the *Phoenix*, which belonged to both Giles and his sister Margaret Brent and was valued at £200. Next, Ingle sacked Margaret's house in St. Mary's, which housed much of her brother's goods, and Giles's house in Kent Island. Between the two locations, he took everything, from account books and silverware to hogs, servants, tobacco, furniture and jewelry made of sapphire and diamonds.[23] But Ingle's depredations did not last forever. With the help of Virginians and Governor Berkeley, Governor Calvert assembled enough men and guns in late 1646 to retake St. Mary's and reclaim the colony.

EDWARD DAVIS, LIONEL DELAWAFER, JOHN HINSON AND PETER CLOISE

On a hot summer day in June 1688, four men—Edward Davis, an enslaved black man named Peter Cloise, Lionel Delawafer and John Hinson—made their way down the Chesapeake in an unassuming shallop.[24] The men were accompanied by a treasure-trove of goods. Davis had three bags of Spanish pieces of eight, 142 pounds of broken silver, silk stockings and expensive linens. Similarly, Delawafer had three bags of Spanish currency, thirty-seven silver plates, silver lace, 84 pounds of broken silver and an assortment of dishes. Hinson had an additional two bags of Spanish currency—including eight hundred pieces of eight—106 pounds worth of broken silver and fine linens and cloth. Altogether, the goods were valued at over £2,300.[25]

So, how did these men come to have such a wealth of belongings? They were former associates of South Sea buccaneer John Cook, whose exploits on the *Revenge* were chronicled in William Dampier's *A New Voyage Round the World*. Cook first gained notoriety as quartermaster of Captain Yankes, the second-highest ranking on a ship, according to the law of privateers. Yankes held a French commission for attacking Spanish ships. After a particularly successful venture, Cook was appointed captain of a prize vessel taken from the Spanish and several of Yankes's men, including Edward Davis. The only problem for Cook and his men, however, was that they didn't have a true commission; this technically made all of their actions those of pirates. Some of the French commanders who had been sailing with Yankes did not appreciate having an Englishman at the helm of their prized ship. So, they rallied together and plundered the English ships, goods and arms. As for the Englishmen, most were marooned on the Isle of Vacca. Meanwhile, Cook, Davis and about eight other men were taken as prisoners to Petit Guavres, but Davis and Cook managed to escape and seized a ship to pick up all of the marooned men. During their departure, Cook and Davis seized another French ship that was laden with wine and goods. Their plan was to embark on their own South Seas adventure, but they first went to Virginia to sell the wine and refit the ships.[26]

Cook and his men made their way to Accomack and used their profits from the wine to buy sails, tackle and all things "necessary for so long a voyage." Most of the men, including Dampier and Davis, remained committed to the new venture. They were also joined by new faces, including Lionel Delawafer and John Hinson. Cook's initial crew consisted of at least seventy men, and they departed for the South Seas in August 1683. For five years, they operated under the guise of privateering and terrorized Spanish outposts, especially those in Panama. After Captain Cook's untimely death from illness in the spring of 1684, Davis (Cook's quartermaster and second-in-command) took over as captain. The men continued to plunder their way around the South Seas in Cook's absence and frequently went back to the Chesapeake to refit their vessels and replenish their supplies. Their numbers continued to grow, and by the end of Davis's piratical career, he commanded over one thousand men and an entire fleet of ships.[27]

After several difficult years, Davis's men decided to retire from committing seaborne crimes and live the rest of their lives in peace and comfort. Unfortunately for them, King James had recently renewed his predecessor's proclamation against piracy. In order to effectively eradicate the issue of piracy in the West Indies, the Crown commissioned Sir Robert Holmes to track down pirates. Holmes's commission placed his authority above that of the English colonial governors in the Atlantic, and he was granted any of the profits he or his agents seized from pirates. Because of this, Holmes took no chances whenever he or his agents crossed paths with a vessel that was unknown to them. One of Holmes's agents, Captain Simon Rowe, witnessed a shallop making its way down the Chesapeake and was immediately suspicious when he saw that it was carrying rather large chests. Rowe ordered the shallop to stop and, upon further inspection, seized the men and their goods and immediately shipped them to Jamestown under suspicion of piracy.[28]

While in Jamestown, the men were independently interrogated by members of the Council in Virginia. Both Delawafer and Hinson denied having known Davis for very long and claimed that they encountered each other in Bermuda. Delawafer and Hinson also denied being privateers or present in the South Seas. Delawafer, for example, claimed that he had spent the last several years in the West Indies and that he sometimes did trade with the Spanish and privateers. However, he claimed that all the goods in his chest had been bequeathed to him and sent by a friend in Lynnhaven. Peter Cloise's testimony was the thing that spelled trouble for the men and undermined their denials. According to Cloise's testimony, all of the men had been plundering together for many years.[29] One has to wonder how much of Cloise's admission was coerced. Regardless, the men began to slightly alter their stories.

They began to claim that, upon their passage between Pennsylvania and Maryland, they had secured certificates of immunity from Captain Thomas Allen of HMS *Quaker* and that Captain Rowe had ignored them.[30] Their arguments proved to be fruitless, and the men were imprisoned in Jamestown. Fortunately for them, however, a lawyer named Micaiah Perry believed that he could get the men out of jail based on the caveat of the 1678 and 1687 proclamation: if a pirate or privateer surrendered within eighteen months of the proclamation, he would receive "full and gracious pardons." In opposition to this argument, Governor Howard said that it was evident that the men had been pirates and that the insistence of their innocence meant that they could not receive the king's pardon. Even if they had admitted to their wicked deeds, it would have meant forfeiture of all the goods and silver they'd acquired, so Perry convinced the men to give up their act of innocence and to apply for the pardon.[31]

Since the men were still concerned about their valuables, they took their lawyer's advice, but they continued to petition for the restoration of their confiscated goods and promised to give £300 of it to the College at Virginia.[32] For several years, the men languished in jail while government officials bickered over the political rulings regarding piracy, pardons and the division or return of seized goods. It ultimately took them three years and a trip to England to retrieve even a fraction of the goods that they'd started with. In the years that had passed, much of their loot had been picked over by various officials, but even still, the men were good on their word and delivered £300 to what is now the College of William and Mary.

ROGER MAKEELE

Not much was known about Roger Makeele before Richard Stevens informed local government officials about his piratical activities along the Accomack. According to Stevens, he and a couple of associates were taking a ship laden with £20,000 worth of tobacco from Choptank to Northampton County in Virginia. As night approached, the men decided to anchor at Gabriell's Island in Watt's Creek to rest. While entertaining themselves by a fire near the boat, they were approached by four very well-armed men who were led by a man named Roger Makeele. Stevens recognized Makeele from previous interactions in the area. Stevens initially tried to fight back but was "violently thrust" into the water. Stevens and his associates were held hostage by Makeele and a few of his men, while several other members of the pirate crew took the tobacco-laden boat to a hiding place on a nearby island. The entire operation took at least two hours. Since it was very late by the time they had finished, Makeele ordered several of his men to keep an armed guard over their vessels and the prisoners while the rest retreated to a house to rest.

The next day, Makeele permitted the men and prisoners to come to the house, where they found the pirates jovial and getting very drunk off of "rumm or brandy." As the pirates drank and ate their fill, their prisoners asked to be relieved, but for two days and two nights, the pirates forced their prisoners to fast and watch on hungrily. Having had his fill of this mild torture, Makeele finally ordered the prisoners be released. He had one of his men place the hostages in a small boat that had been hidden in the brush and take them to the mainland, where the men were left in a remote, marshy area. To add insult to injury, Makeele's agent forced the men to give up their clothing as a form of payment for the boat ride, despite the cold January temperatures. Stevens made his way back to Accomack, but he believed his associates might have gone to Dorchester (Dorsett) County.

Not even a week later, Makeele and his men attempted to seize another vessel, a sloop carrying £800 to £900 worth of goods that was making its way from the Western to the Eastern Shore. The crew of this ship also decided to weigh anchor for the night at Watt's Creek. Once they landed, two of the crewmembers decided to head to shore, where they came upon Makeele and his men. This time, Makeele invited the men and their associates to join them. He told them that they could refresh themselves with rum, fresh beef and mutton. Most fortunately for the men, another merchant ship was nearby; it was in poor condition and carrying only lumber, but its captain knew Makeele and his plans for the unsuspecting crew. So, rather than join Makeele for refreshments, the men hastily made their way back to their vessel and sailed away before they could be captured.[33] But this was only the beginning of Makeele's depredations.

Credible reports suggest that Makeele and his "confederacy" of pirates not only attempted to attack several vessels, but they even took to plundering on dry land. They attacked the local indigenous population and robbed them of their guns, furs and other precious items.

Over a month after Makeele was first reported for his piratical acts, the Governor's Council issued a warrant for the arrest of him and his associates. Since Makeele was an inhabitant of Virginia, the council reached out to Virginia officials for assistance in capturing him. After Maryland and Virginia joined forces to capture him, Makeele fled to the safer, shallow sounds and rivers of North Carolina. There is no record of what happened to Makeele after he fled the Chesapeake, and his name was never again uttered in the region. We can speculate that he was eventually captured, killed or simply retired his pirating lifestyle.[34]

JOHN JAMES

Perhaps one of the biggest threats to the Chesapeake Bay region was the ruthless mutineer John James. Like most other pirates, there are no records of his life before he turned up in depositions from the summer of 1699. James began his piratical career as a member of a multinational crew under the command of a Dutchman named Captain Hind. Near the end of April 1699, Hind and his men planned an attack against a twenty-two-gun frigate they had encountered. The *Providence*, as the frigate was called, was commanded by Captain William Rhett of South Carolina.[35] Although the ship put up a good fight, it was "outdone and taken" by Hind, and his men added yet another vessel to their little convoy. But Hind wouldn't get to enjoy his prize for long, as the Englishmen aboard the *Providence* mutinied and seized the vessel. After the Englishmen gained control of the ship, John James was immediately made captain.

James was described as a man of average height with broad shoulders and "large joints." His face was menacing and incredibly disfigured from smallpox, and he was thick lipped with a blemish in his eye. Because he was so physically intimidating, it's easy to see how the mutineers chose him to be their new leader. James's first act as captain was to maroon Captain Hind and fifteen of his men on an island ten leagues from New Providence. One can imagine what he expected the marooned men to do after he left them with "three small arms and a bottle of gunpowder." After leaving the men on the island, James and his men took the *Providence* to the island of New Providence and held several locals hostage until his ship was fully refitted, restocked and repaired.

With a well-armed and replenished ship, the men began pirating on their own terms. There are a number of accounts of James's exploits from Lynnhaven Bay and the surrounding area. Their first success in the Chesapeake region was the sacking of the pink *Hope*, which was headed for London at the time. The ship was rather inconsequential aside from the six months of record books belonging to HMS *Essex Prize* that it was carrying. After capturing the ship, James's men interrogated its crew in order to substantiate the information found within the record books. They learned strategic information, including the weaknesses in Virginia and Maryland's defenses, as well as the number of crewmembers aboard the *Essex Prize*. Perhaps most importantly, the record books noted that the *Essex Prize* was the only man-of-war defending the entirety of the Chesapeake. The potential of lucrative prizes was too tantalizing to pass up. James recognized that his own ship, the *Alexander*, was better equipped than the *Essex*, with twenty-six guns and a force of 150 men (HMS *Essex* only had sixteen guns and 70 men), so to him, attacking the ship was a no-brainer. The men volleyed shot after shot at each other for a mere four hours before the *Essex* lost over half of its crew and was forced to flee. Reports say that James and his crewmembers were determined to remain in the bay to take better ships and grow their fleet.

During their attack on the *Essex Prize*, the *Providence*, which James had renamed the *Alexander*, came across a ship from Bristol, the *Maryland Merchant*, that was trying to enter the James River. It was entirely too easy for the men to turn their attention to the small *Maryland Merchant*. When James boarded the ship, he told the captain, Burgess, that he was a friend to the English nation. Although James's needs would be met, he said, he was willing to pay for whatever supplies the men seized. James's men boasted to Burgess that they had over £3 million worth of gold and silver in their hold. They stripped the small merchant ship of its sailing gear and one hundred pounds of dry goods. Seeing that the captain of the *Maryland Merchant* had less than £100 in plate, James opted not to rob Burgess but ultimately refused to pay for the items he confiscated. Before his departure from the small vessel, James insisted that he was Captain Kidd. His ruse worked, and the master of the vessel testified that although the crew called him John James, "from the description [he had] of him in the country, he [was] said to be Kidd." After their raid of the *Maryland Merchant*, James and his men took on a sloop that was carrying corn and pork from North Carolina. Joseph Baker of the

Charles from New York and John Mitchell of an unnamed sloop both testified that James had plundered their ships and robbed them clean.

Micaiah made another appearance to warn those trading in Virginia and Maryland of the imminent dangers they faced in the Chesapeake. No fewer than thirty ships were seized by pirates in the region within three months. Another ship, the *Roanoke Merchant*, soon became a victim of Captain James's tyranny. The ship belonged to Colonel Robert Quary, the judge of the admiralty for the southern colonies, and its commander, Captain Jones, made his way through the Virginia Capes into Lynnhaven Bay. He saw the *Alexander* nearby but mistook it for the *Essex Prize* and believed it was the guardship of the region. But Captain Jones was sorely mistaken, and after firing just two shots, Captain James commanded Jones to come aboard the *Alexander*. What ensued was several days of torture and humiliation, as James enjoyed playing mind games. He threatened Jones and his crewmembers with impressment and forced him to beg for his life and freedom. Ultimately, James released the *Roanoke Merchant* but not before plundering it of the majority of its cargo, including pork, tallow, guns, carpenters' tools, water and animal skins. James also filled Jones's and his men's heads with misinformation; for example, he told them that they had a consort sloop of eight guns and fifty men lurking somewhere in the Chesapeake. Upon his release, Jones made his way to Annapolis, and once he was in Maryland, he reported his experience directly to Governor Blakiston.

After hearing of Captain Jones's ordeal from Governor Blakiston, Lord Bellomont was determined to deal with James and sent Captain Crow and the *Arundel* to capture the menace. Although James and his crew had long "infested" the Chesapeake, they fled before Captain Crow could make good on his commission. That was the last that was ever heard of Captain James in the records.[36]

CAPTAIN KIDD

As ships made their way down the River Thames and locals strolled the streets along its banks, their eyes and noses were met with a grisly scene. Dangling above them were the black, decaying bodies of pirates whose marauding had earned them the hangman's noose instead of the king's pardon. Most of the corpses were those of nameless, simple seamen whose role in piratical sea-roving was not large enough to warrant broadsides (a large printed sheet used for announcements) and ballads. But in May 1699, one body garnered significant attention: that of Captain William Kidd. His death ended over a decade of devastations. His exploits were well known among merchants and government officials, but his reputation exploded with the publication of two broadsides. The first gave an account of his hanging day, and the second was a ballad that celebrated his piratical career.[37]

Aside from his birth in Scotland, little is known about Kidd's early life. His career took him from being a seaman's apprentice to a member of a pirate ship and then from privateer and pirate hunter to pirate captain. So, how did he become one of the most notorious figures of the Indo-Atlantic world? Kidd first appears in the official record in 1689 at forty-four years of age, when he was a member of a pirate crew. For reasons unknown, Kidd was part of a mutiny on that ship; he stole the vessel and took it to the island of Nevis, where it was renamed the *Blessed William*. At the time of the mutiny, England was in the midst of a major conflict with the French as part of the Nine Years' War (1688–1697). Christopher Codrington, the governor of Nevis, hoped to use the men aboard the *Blessed William* to his advantage and to protect the Caribbean islands under English control from French incursions. The *Blessed William*, under the command of Captain Kidd, was refitted and joined a larger squadron of ships. This squadron was to be commanded by a Royal Navy captain, but Codrington lacked the funds to pay the privateers their wages. Instead, their pay would come from whatever prize they took from the French.[38]

One of their first adventures was to the French island Mariegalante, a Leeward Island in the Lesser Antilles. There, the squadron destroyed the only town on the island, burned down all of the sugar plantations and plundered every possible item they could as a means of payment. At that point, Kidd's men were pleased with their marauding; in the hold of the *Blessed William* was at least £2,000 worth of loot. But when they realized that they would also be used to attack French naval vessels—that had no goods or money to plunder—they became agitated. When they returned to Nevis, the men mutinied and Kidd rowed to shore. Although Kidd lost a significant chunk of change, Governor Codrington was happy with his performance in the conflict.[39] Kidd was granted a new vessel, the *Antigua*, for his actions against the French, and he was granted a commission to seek out the *Blessed William* and its mutinous crew. He heard that the crew had a design to head to New York after looting several Spanish ships. New York ports had a reputation for being pirate havens for refitting and selling stolen goods at market. Unfortunately for Kidd, he never caught up to the vessel.

The Tryal of Captain WILLIAM KIDD, Page 451.
for Murder and Pyracy, upon Six seve-
ral Indictments. As also, the Tryals
of NICHOLAS CHURCHILL, JAMES
HOW, ROBERT LAMLEY, WILLIAM
JENKINS, GABRIEL LOFF, HUGH
PARROT, RICHARD BARLICORN,
ABEL OWENS, *and* DARBY MULLINS,
for Pyracy; at the Admiralty Sessions
held at the Old-Bailey, *the 8th and 9th*
of May, 13 W. III. 1701.

THE first Indictment against *William Kidd,*   Page 453.
was for Murder, and sets forth; " That the The first In-
" said *William Kidd,* not having the Fear of God dictment a-
" before his Eyes, &c. the 30th of *October,* in gainst *Kidd,*
" the 9th Year of the King, by Force and Arms, for murdering
" upon the High Sea, near the Coast of *Mala-* *William Moor*
" bar, in the *East-Indies,* and within the Jurisdi- his Gunner.
" ction of the Admiralty of *England*; in a cer-
" tain Ship, call'd the *Adventure Galley,* whereof
" the said *William Kidd* was then Commander;
" did, of his Malice aforethought, then, and there,
" make an Assault, in and upon one *William*
" *Moor,* then belonging to the said *Adventure*
" *Galley*: And the said *William Kidd,* with a cer-
" tain wooden Bucket, bound with Iron Hoops,
Vol. IV. Part I.   M m   did

The Tryal of Captain Kidd for Murder and Pyracy, circa 1701. *Courtesy of the Library of Congress Law Library.*

While in New York, Kidd had the opportunity to settle down for a time as the husband of the extremely wealthy widow Sarah Bradley Cox Oort. The couple obtained their marriage license just days after Oort's second husband had died, which led to suspicions that the two had been having an affair and that Kidd led the unsuspecting John Oort to his untimely death. But in 1695, Kidd grew tired of the settled lifestyle and plotted a way to return to his former privateering ways. The war between England and France was still raging, and English shipping was suffering at the hands of pirates and French privateers. So, Kidd set off for London in the *Antigua* to seek a new commission.[40]

With years of experience, intimate knowledge of pirates and the backing of some wealthy and powerful individuals, Kidd easily secured his desired commissions and a new ship called the *Adventure Galley*. His first commission, which was granted in December 1695, gave him the authority to disrupt enemy shipping. His second, granted in January 1696, enabled him to seek out and seize pirates of any nation, including England. After obtaining commissions and a ship, all Kidd had to do was put together a crew of at least one hundred men under the rule of "no purchase, no pay." This, again, meant that the men would not be paid a wage but would be paid via whatever booty they secured from the ships they seized.[41] Additionally, Kidd agreed to pay £20,000 should he not return with the promised loot by March 1697. But he would be rewarded with ownership of the *Adventure Galley* if he and his crew seized at least £100,000 in prizes. So, with the success of his commission and his ability to pay his crew hanging on whether or not he could attack enough French ships or seize enough pirates, Kidd set sail in April 1696.

Kidd was under enormous pressure to be successful, so he stacked his crew with former pirates and privateers who he believed would benefit him. Within several months, his voyage seemed doomed to fail; about half of his crew was sick and dying, and his ship was leaking. They'd only managed to seize a single French ship, his crew was becoming mutinous and Kidd nearly lost it all when, in November 1697, he came across a merchantman under the command of an English captain whose pass he found to be legitimate. The ship belonged to Madras (Chennai) in India, which was not an enemy of the English, and therefore, Kidd and his men had no authority to seize it. But when his men heard that there were "precious stones and other rich goods on board," they were determined to take it. However, Kidd prevailed and the men moved on.[42]

Kidd's luck changed on the first day of February 1698, when he and his men came across a merchant ship called the *Quedah Merchant*. At the time, the *Quedah Merchant* was bound from Surat to the Spice Islands with a cargo of silk, cloth, sugar, opium and other goods that was valued at £30,000. Kidd, with a design to trick the other vessel, hoisted French colors; he intercepted the ship, which also raised French flags. The *Quedah Merchant*'s captain was summoned to the *Adventure Galley*, but the captain was an Englishman and, fearing a misunderstanding, sent one of his Frenchmen over with their pass. This pass was from the French East India Company, and Kidd knew this would be a lawful prize. It was at this point that Kidd raised the English colors and seized the *Quedah Merchant*, which he renamed the *Adventure Merchant*.[43]

Kidd continued to cruise the region and search for loot. At one point, he came upon the *Mocha Frigate*, a pirate ship under command of Robert Culliford. Kidd claimed that he tried to seize the vessel but that his men threatened to shoot him, so he let the pirates go. He also came across several ships that belonged to the Dutch, Portuguese and the East India Company. Since these ships were unlawful prizes, Kidd claimed that his crew forced him to seize them under the threat of a mutiny. But to English authorities, it seemed that Kidd was ultimately using his commission as a means to attack not only French ships but those of the Dutch, Spanish, Portuguese and Moors.[44] Although Kidd operated out of Madagascar and most of his exploits took place in the Red Sea and Indian Ocean, by the end of the 1690s, the mere mention of his name was enough to send the Chesapeake into a serious panic. Kidd had made many friends in the Caribbean, and he provided them with a "great quantity of money" and "several goods," but English authorities and many in the Chesapeake were worried that they would suffer significant losses at his hands.[45] In the spring of 1699, the English authorities ordered all colonial governors, including those of Virginia (Nicholson) and Maryland (Blakiston), to be on the lookout for Kidd and his *Adventure Prize*.[46]

In the summer of 1699, reports noted that one of Kidd's ships was trying to unload a quantity of silver plate and gold from Delaware to the Chesapeake. Not long after the governors had received their directives and dispatched colonial agents to seek out pirates in the region, Governor Nicholson of Virginia, a native of Accomack County, learned that Kidd had landed a forty-two-gun ship and an eighteen-gun sloop in Accomack on the Eastern Shore. Virginians and Marylanders began posting pirate lookouts, and patrols were set up to find Kidd before he could land in the colony. It was reported that locals were visiting Kidd's ships that were rumored to be filled with an enormous amount of gold and jewels worth no less than £520,000.

For a while, it seemed that Virginia might become a refuge for pirates who had sailed with Kidd, as over sixty of his men reportedly settled in the area after deserting him. Accomack, it seemed, was an ideal location for Kidd to fence his loot, as he could easily get out into the safety of the open waters of the Atlantic. The residents there also appeared to be friendly to pirates visiting the Eastern Shore. But it wasn't just Kidd who found

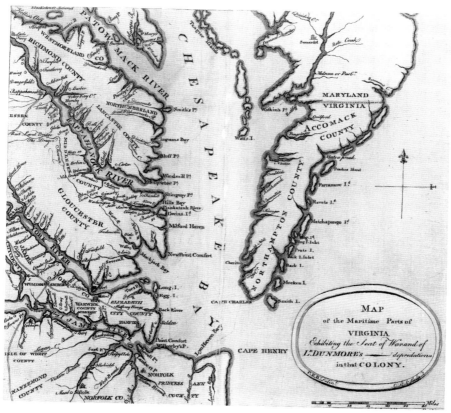

Map of the maritime parts of Virginia, circa 1776. *Courtesy of the Library of Congress Geography and Map Division.*

refuge in Accomack; nearly one hundred pirates and deserters made the broader Chesapeake region their home. Government officials and the local inhabitants of Maryland and Virginia began to feel that they were under direct threat; the Chesapeake's northern neighbors even asked for their help with men-of-war as a means of protection. Kidd, however, quickly made his way from Virginia up the coastline to Pennsylvania, Delaware and New York. He reportedly hid his fortune along the way. His final destination was Boston, Massachusetts, where he was arrested and sent to England to await trial. On May 23, 1701, Kidd ultimately met his fate at the end of a hangman's noose.[47]

THEOPHILUS TURNER

Some people are born to live a life of crime, while others find themselves thrown into it. Theophilus Turner, much like many others, didn't start out as a pirate, and his piratical adventures proved to be short-lived. At the age of twenty-seven, Turner was working as a joiner aboard a thirty-two-gun merchant ship called the *Hannibal*. Under the command of William Hill, Turner, along with 70 other men, experienced a miserable existence; their pay was often withheld, and they were punished for minor offences. While resupplying on the coast of Guinea, several of the men aboard the *Hannibal* planned a mutiny. While Turner didn't admit to participating in the mutiny, he did remain on the vessel when it left Guinea and ventured to Brazil. In 1699, after spending what must have been a grueling year living in Brazil, Turner was once again employed as a joiner. In the same year, a French vessel with a destroyed mast arrived in Brazil. When the ship was restored to mint condition, it set sail for Bengal on the coast of India, but it never made it to its destination. When the ship stopped on an island near Madagascar, off the coast of Africa, its crew was met by a forty-gun pirate ship called the *Resolution*. The ship was carrying at least 130 pirates under the command of Captain Robert Culliford, the very Culliford who had stolen his ship from the infamous Captain Kidd. Although the men aboard the *Hannibal* tried to escape the pirates, they were easily overtaken. Turner was the only Englishman on board, so he was brought before Culliford to give an account of the vessel's cargo.

With his life threatened, Turner quickly told the pirates about the wine, cloth and nearly £2,000 worth of currency aboard the ship. Since Turner was the only Englishman on board, Culliford refused to let him go. Culliford and his men pillaged their way from the Indian Ocean to the coast of Rhode Island, where they met up with another pirate, Richard Chivers, who had about eighty or ninety men at his command aboard a twelve-gun vessel. The men then decided to plunder their way back toward the coast of India, where they met again near Surat. Working in concert, Culliford and Chivers attacked a Turkish ship that was carrying various forms of currency valued between £120,000 and £130,000. Only a few shots were exchanged before the pirates boarded the vessel and seized all of the currency. After dividing the loot among themselves, each pirate was awarded between £700 and £800. Even Turner, as a prisoner, was awarded a modest sum of £250 for his assistance on board the ship (although some reports believe that he received the same share as the rest of the crew).

Turner was granted the opportunity to join the pirates on their next adventure, but he somehow skipped out on Culliford's crew and found himself on board another pirate ship called the *Nassau*, which was under the command of Giles Shelley, a former member of Captain Kidd's crew. The *Nassau* had made its way from Madagascar to the capes of Delaware; while prowling the coast, they attacked a ship under the command of Captain Gravenrod, who was asked to take Turner and several other pirates on board. Some of the unknown pirates were then transferred to another ship bound for England, but Turner opted to remain with Gravenrod and live out his days in anonymity in Maryland. But a wrench was thrown into Turner's plans when Maryland governor Nathaniel Blakiston received word of their imminent arrival. As Gravenrod navigated the Severn River, one of Blakiston's agents seized the vessel and brought the men to prison. While he was imprisoned, Turner offered to confess how he'd come to join these desperate rogues and gave an account of the pirates in Madagascar whose plan it was to attack merchant ships from New York to Carolina in exchange for mercy. Blakiston believed Turner's "ingenious and genuine" confession and requested the king's mercy when he sent Turner to London to stand trial. However, Turner's ultimate fate is unknown.[48]

LOUIS (LEWIS) GUITTAR

The sun was slowly setting when, in the spring of 1700, Captain William Passenger of HMS *Shoreham* heard from a local merchant that a pirate was hanging out in Lynnhaven Bay.[49] The pirate was said to be attacking vessels laden with valuable goods as they went through the bay, including a Barbadian sugar vessel. It was also said that he had taken many locals hostage. The pirate turned out to be a Frenchman named Captain Louis Guittar; his vessel, *La Paix* (The Peace), weighed two hundred tons and held at least twenty guns and nearly 150 men. It was feared that, unless swift action was taken, the pirate would do more harm and continue to increase his strength. Before he was captured, Guittar seized no fewer than three vessels in a single week. On April 17, 1700, he took a pink called the *Baltimore*; the pirates kept the ship, killed one man and kidnapped the other twelve on board. Guittar kept six men on the pink, along with sixteen members of his crew, and brought the other six on board *La Paix*. On the following day, the men took a sloop called the *George* and imprisoned its captain and crew. They plundered the vessel of its goods, including £200 worth of gold, and added it to their growing fleet. On April 23, Guittar and his men seized the *Pennsylvania Merchant*, an eighty-ton vessel bound for Philadelphia from London. Following a familiar pattern, the pirates boarded the ship, kidnapped all thirty-one crewmembers and rifled the ship. They took the personal belongings of the crew, including a green and gold enameled watch, and all the sails, rigging, spars, et cetera from the ship itself. This time, however, they also burned the ship. In the following weeks, they continued their pillaging pattern and attacked the *Indian King*, the *Friendship of Belfast*, the *Nicholson* and an unknown pink. While they didn't keep all of the ships as part of their fleet, they gained five new vessels in addition to *La Paix*.[50]

Passenger received a letter from the governor seeking his assistance in dealing with the pirates aboard *La Paix*. The governor of Virginia (and former governor of Maryland), Francis Nicholson, had made it his mission to eradicate piracy in the Chesapeake, and he urged government officials in England to send several men-of-war to the Chesapeake to protect Virginia and Maryland. The *Shoreham* was one of these war vessels. In the mayor's letter to Passenger, he ordered the ship to sail as soon as it was ready and the weather was favorable. Additionally, Nicholson authorized Passenger to stop all ships from entering or leaving the capes in his pursuit of the pirate, and he left it to their discretion whether they burned, took or sank the pirate ship. Furthermore, Nicholson ordered that anyone who seized or killed one of these pirates would be awarded twenty pounds.[51]

Despite contrary winds, Passenger anchored the *Shoreham* just three leagues short of Guittar's location. At around 10:00 p.m. that night, Governor Nicholson joined Passenger on the *Shoreham*, though it's unclear whether Nicholson simply wanted to make sure that this new thorn in his side was dealt with or if he had a taste for adventure himself. Either way, he remained on board the ship for the entirety of the ensuing conflict. Passenger's men rested before making their next move. At about 4:00 a.m., Passenger sailed within a half mile of the pirate; Guittar spotted them and immediately turned to attack. He reportedly said, "This is but a small fellow; we shall have him presently," and attempted to get in position to board the *Shoreham*. But Passenger anticipated the pirates' design and fired a single shot at the ship. In response, Guittar raised his flag—a Jack with a broad red pendant—and returned the favor.

Guittar's ship had a significant force of men and guns, but Passenger was also well equipped. The ships exchanged gunfire for nearly ten hours at "pistol shot" distance from each other. At 3:00 p.m., the wind picked up, and Passenger, "sailing something better than the pirate," outmaneuvered Guittar. His actions prevented the pirates from boarding the *Shoreham*, and in the hours of gunfire exchanged between the two vessels, Passenger managed to shatter all the masts and riggings of the pirate ship, destroy several of its guns and all but gut its hull. As the pirate ship tried to escape, it found itself too close to the shore, and without braces, bowlines or sails, the vessel crashed into the shore. But rather than surrender to Passenger, the pirates laid a line of gunpowder to thirty whole barrels of additional gunpowder. They threatened to blow the ship up with the hostages still inside. One of the prisoners, when he heard the pirates' plan, begged them to let him go to Passenger and request quarter for them. Governor Nicholson, who was concerned about the well-being of his majesty's subjects, agreed; as long as the pirates quietly turned themselves in, Nicholson would refer them to the king's mercy.

In all, 124 pirates were taken prisoner—the vast majority of them were French or Dutch. Some of them, however, were local boys; the pilot, John Hoogley, hailed from New York but was of Dutch parentage. A total of 111 of these men were sent to England to await the king's judgment. Additionally, between 25 and 30 had been killed in the fighting, 3 were executed in Virginia and between 40 and 50 hostages were recovered. In the cold winter air, blackened corpses hung high along the River Thames. Each rotting corpse represented a pirate who failed to receive the mercy of the king's pardon. This was a grisly reminder to sailors of what the consequences were for becoming a pirate. Many of those who were hanging in the winter and spring of 1701 were the Frenchmen from *La Paix*. In a single day, Guittar and 23 of his men were hanged. Clearly, the king was feeling less than charitable.[52]

BLACK SAM BELLAMY

The late summer sun shone brightly overhead. Two men kept watch over the Spaniards, who were quickly salvaging as much as they could from a recent wreck off the coast of Florida. The coast of Florida was prime hunting ground, as Spanish ships were prone to wrecking among the many reefs and sand banks. But Sam Bellamy and his partner Paul Williams were, once again, too late to secure anything that had significant value.[53] They then had to wait for the Spaniards to finish for the day before they could sneak in and scavenge the rest. This was the last time that they would be left with a paltry sum. The two decided that the only way they were going to make their fortune was to "go upon the account," a phrase commonly used among the pirates. Rather than scavenging the wreckage, they would go straight to the source.

Very little information about Bellamy's life before he turned to crime in 1717 exists, although he did tell one victim that he was an Englishman, born of London. After he and Williams came into the possession of two vessels, the two went hunting. In February 1717, the two men encountered their first victim: a galley called the *Whidah*. It was a three-hundred-ton vessel mounted with eighteen guns, but it was only carrying 50 men. The ship had incredibly valuable cargo, which included elephants' teeth (ivory), gold dust, sugar, indigo and other "rich merchandize" bound for London. Bellamy and Williams took the risk and chased the vessel for three days before the *Whidah* finally surrendered. Bellamy's next move earned him a reputation for being merciful and generous. He exchanged his own ship, the *Sultana*, for the *Whidah* and released its crew without injury. Bellamy then added ten additional guns and a crew of 150 to 200 men from all nations, including 25 formerly enslaved black men. The *Whidah* was joined by Williams's eight-gun sloop and 80 men. Unlike most pirates who operated out of the Caribbean islands, Bellamy decided that they should infest the waters of the Chesapeake, especially those off the coast of Virginia.[54]

Before they were able to reach the American coastline, they were swept up in a terrible tempest. As the skies opened up, a "thunder shower overtook them with such violence" that the *Whidah* nearly toppled over. A changing of the winds saved the men from certain death, but as the night approached, the storm's intensity increased. The wind roared, lightning flashed and thunder clapped incessantly at a volume that was "sufficient to strike a dread of the supream [*sic*] being, who commands the sea and the winds." But Bellamy's men shouted "blasphemies, oaths and horrid imprecations to drown the uproar of jarring elements." Bellamy believed the gods must have gotten drunk on their tipple to cause such a storm. After four days and three nights, the storm "abated of its fury," and the skies cleared. The men were happy to find that the *Whidah* experienced minimal damage, losing only its mainsail, and they continued their course. While cruising off the coast of Rhode Island, the men came across a sloop commanded by Captain Beers. Bellamy and Williams decided to return the vessel to Beers only after they had already plundered it of its cargo, but their men would hear nothing of the sort and sank the vessel instead.[55]

Before Beers was dropped at Block Island, it is reported that Bellamy said, "D—n my Bl—d…I scorn to do any one a mischief, when it is not for my advantage." Bellamy then went on a tirade about the corruption of the world and how "[pirates] rob the poor under the cover of law, forsooth, and we plunder the rich under the protection of our own courage." This was the first—but not the last—time that Bellamy likened himself to Robin Hood.[56] Over the next few weeks, Bellamy and his crew sacked countless ships, and they soon recognized that many of the vessels leaving the Chesapeake were laden with heavy hogsheads of tobacco. Hogsheads could be difficult to move, were too bulky for pirate vessels and were not easy to market in the colonies. The inbound ships, however, were typically filled with rich cargo from Europe and the West Indies, which included porcelain, silk, sugar, rum and other miscellaneous items. These goods were much more marketable in the colonies and were easier to transport on the smaller pirate ships.

On April 7, 1717, near Cape Charles in the Chesapeake, Bellamy and his crew plundered the *Agnis*, which was bound from Jamaica and filled with rum, sugar and molasses, and took the ship. On the same day, they plundered the *Anne Galley*—which Bellamy kept—and the *Endeavor*, and on April 12, they captured a vessel from Leith, Scotland. All four vessels were bound for Virginia at the time of their attacks.[57] In the meantime, Williams had also been successfully plundering the Chesapeake. Since he had a smaller vessel, he was able to navigate the many inlets and islets at the mouth of the bay and watch for incoming maritime traffic. On April 9, Williams watched as a ship sailed into the capes, and with the element of surprise, he quickly overtook it without so much as a shot fired. The ship was called the *Tryal*, and Williams's men spent hours looting their prize. When Williams saw a strange sail entering the area, he demanded that the captain, John Lucas, follow him as they fled. But when Lucas had the chance, he escaped into the capes and got away from the pirates.[58]

After their early April ventures, the two captains reunited. The *Whidah* was in need of cleaning, and the men were in need of rest. Escorted by the *Anne Galley*, the pirates entered the Chesapeake yet again to find an isolated location to careen. At that point, Bellamy heard that a guardship, HMS *Shoreham*, had been dispatched to the region to root out pirates. After sighting a large ship in Lynnhaven Bay, Bellamy became concerned about being captured and ordered the pirate convoy to flee. Bellamy had no idea that the *Shoreham* was actually off the coast of South Carolina at the time. After fleeing the bay, Williams and Bellamy were separated by a storm, never to be reunited again. On April 27, Bellamy and his crew came across a ship bound for New England from the Madeiras, which they seized near Cape Cod. They took the master and all but two of the crewmen from the vessel and held them as prisoners on the *Whidah*. Seven of Bellamy's men were sent over to guard their prize and the two additional prisoners.

To celebrate yet another success, the men on each ship helped themselves to the large quantities of wine and alcohol that was on board the captured vessel. When the two prisoners on board the captured ship saw the pirates drunkenly passed out on the deck, they took the opportunity and steered the ship toward the land, running it aground quickly. Local inhabitants helped the two men seize the pirates. The pirates were then sent to Boston. When the men on the *Whidah* saw that their prize was getting away, they made chase. But they, too, were entirely too drunk and ran their own vessel aground on the shore south of the Cape. Between 120 and 130 of the ship's crewmembers drowned.

Sam Bellamy and his few surviving crewmembers were imprisoned, condemned and executed for piracy. They met their maker at the end of the hangman's noose.[59] Before he died, Sam Bellamy was reported to be the wealthiest pirate in recorded history. He plundered at least fifty-three ships in a single year.

RICHARD WORLEY

There were eight resolute men who wanted to go pirating, so they set sail in a small boat with a handful of biscuits, a small cask of water and maybe half a dozen old muskets. The sight of them would have hardly struck fear in the hearts of anyone, but size didn't matter to Richard Worley and his men. Realizing that their vessel was not equipped for any great adventure, they kept to the rivers, inlets and islets. The men left New York in the latter part of September 1718 and made their way along the coastline to the Delaware River. It was there that the men spotted their first prize. Near Newcastle, a shallop carrying plates, household goods and other commodities was bound for Philadelphia when it unwittingly crossed paths with the pirates. The pirates used the element of surprise and boarded the shallop before plundering its more valuable cargo. They also took several of the captain's men, including two black men, from the shallop. Fortunately for the shallop's captain, the pirates let the vessel go.

The captain immediately made his way to Philadelphia to inform the government of what had transpired. This news, along with the presence of other villains like Edward Teach (also known as Blackbeard), was enough to strike fear in the hearts of the authorities. They responded as if a war had been declared and immediately sent dispatches to the colonies between New York and North Carolina. They also sent several men-of-war in search of the rogues but to no avail. Worley and his men were moving down the river, committing their small-scale plunders, when they met a sloop from Philadelphia that belonged to a man of mixed race who they called Black Robbin. This time, Worley and his men ditched their own boat, preferring this new ship instead. They also took one of Black Robbin's men. A couple of days later, they took yet another sloop; this was an even better ship that was filled with provisions and other necessities. It was much better suited, they believed, to their pirating needs.

Although Worley's attacks were relatively small, their successes were large enough to have the local governor issue a proclamation to apprehend all pirates who failed or refused to surrender themselves by the deadline of the king's own proclamation of pardon. While the authorities were beginning to realize that this menace was not the indomitable Blackbeard, the fact that Worley had built success upon success was worrisome. The governor then ordered HMS *Phoenix*, a twenty-gun vessel, to cruise the coastline in search of the villains. Yet luck continued to be on Worley's side, and with their new, better-equipped ship, Worley and his men decided to take to the open ocean. The *Phoenix* was looking for a coast-bound ship, and it happened to miss Worley's ship at the height of the panic. For about six weeks, Worley and his men cruised the open waters and seized a sloop and a brigantine. They burned the sloop since it was from New York, and they feared that word would reach home that Worley was returning to his old stomping grounds. Upon his homecoming, Worley had increased the size of his crew to twenty men, added six guns to his ship and had all the small arms he and his men needed to carry out an assault.

With everything coming up roses for Worley, it was time for him to make his mark. He designed a black flag with a "white Death's Head in the middle of it," and his men signed new articles swearing to fight to the death and take no quarter. Old plans became new again as the men decided to terrorize the shipping lanes between Virginia and New York. They then sold their stolen goods in the ports of Baltimore, Philadelphia and New York City. The pirates realized they needed to clean and refit their ships before taking on their next target, so they pulled into an inlet in North Carolina to make themselves ready. The governor, however, heard of their arrival and sent out two sloops to deal with Worley. One sloop held eight guns, while the other held six, and there were at least seventy-five men divided between the two vessels. Worley narrowly escaped yet again, as he had finished his preparations just before the two sloops arrived. But this time, his escape was short lived.

The two sloops that the governor had prepared were designed to be as inconspicuous as possible and resembled the very merchant ships that Worley was so fond of attacking. While taking the same course as Worley, the sloops intersected him as he and his crewmembers were cruising off the capes of Virginia. Worley turned to make his move and was hoping to cut them off at the James River, just as he'd done many times before. He hoisted his menacing black flag, expecting a quick surrender. The two sloops then quickly raised the king's colors and fired a shot at him. Worley immediately recognized his mistake; the tide had turned against him. Instead of him keeping the sloops from getting into the river, they were blocking him from getting out.

Worley and his men prepared a desperate defense, remembering their blood-sworn oath. As the two sloops from Carolina came broadside and boarded Worley's ship, Worley and his men raised their swords and fought hard. They dashed and slashed, fighting to the death. All of the men perished aside from Worley and one of his crewmen. Both were severely wounded, but that didn't stop the authorities from sending them to the gallows. On February 17, 1719, the bodies of Worley and his last man swayed in the Chesapeake breeze.[60]

BLACKBEARD

Although John James may have proven himself to be the biggest threat to the Chesapeake, there is one figure who looms much larger in the historical record: Blackbeard. Blackbeard was one of the most nefarious pirates who infested the colonial coastline in the early eighteenth century. Some say that he got his start privateering in Jamaica while he was fighting in the war against the French. He was well known for his beard, which was black as tar, nearly as long as his waist, filled with ribbons and "twisted into small tails." He also had menacing eyes that were framed by thick black brows. Blackbeard was known to be heavily armed and often wore a sling that held three pistols. He also reportedly placed "loosely-twisted hemp cord

Page 70

Blackbeard the Pirate.

An illustration of Blackbeard the pirate from Captain Charles Johnson's *A General History of the Pyrates*, 1725. *Courtesy of the Library of Congress Rare Book and Special Collections Division.*

matches, dipped in saltpetre and lime water," under his hat on either side of his head; during battle, he would light the matches, which made him infinitely more terrifying.[61]

Blackbeard first appears in the records as a member of Captain Benjamin Hornigold's crew. Hornigold saw Blackbeard's pirating potential and awarded him a sloop that they'd previously taken as a prize. Most of Blackbeard's early attacks occurred in the West Indies. One particular victimized vessel was bound for South Carolina and filled with goods that were of considerable value. Blackbeard and Hornigold often returned to the coast of Virginia to clean their vessels. When they captured a French guineaman bound for Martinique, Hornigold offered the vessel to Blackbeard. After this particular venture, Hornigold surrendered to authorities. Blackbeard refused, however, and struck out on his own on his new guineaman. It was aboard this ship, which he named the *Queen Anne's Revenge*, that he would mount forty guns. Blackbeard and his men plundered several ships in the meantime and often marooned the crew on shore and burned the ships after they'd gotten what they needed. At one point, Blackbeard even joined up with the gentleman pirate, Stede Bonnet. After cruising the West Indies for many months, the men made their way back to the American coastline and plundered ships from Boston to Charleston, often in revenge for the actions taken against them and former crewmembers.

In June 1718, a letter from Robert Johnson, the governor of South Carolina, sent chills down the spine of every nearby colonial governor, including those of Virginia and Maryland. He recounted how twice, in just nine months, all of the ships entering and leaving the port of Charleston were plundered mercilessly at the hands of one pirate, and that earlier that month, the pirates had struck again. That time, they didn't seize a merchant vessel or one with valuable commodities—no—they took a pilot boat carrying "severall of the best inhabitants" of Charleston and held them hostage. The pirates sent word to the governor that if he did not immediately send chests of medicine, they would murder every single prisoner. The governor, knowing this to be a certainty, sent the requested medicine (worth between £300 and £400). The pirates were merciful, and they didn't murder the important residents of Charleston. Instead, Blackbeard humiliated them by robbing them of all their personal effects, which were worth upward of £1,500. He also forced them to row themselves to shore practically naked. The governor reported that Blackbeard had a ship with more than forty guns and three sloops as part of his convoy. Between the vessels, there were over four hundred men; this was one of the largest pirate crews in the Atlantic.[62]

After securing what they needed off the coast of South Carolina, Blackbeard and his crew made their way to North Carolina and Virginia, where they plundered several more vessels. Blackbeard knew that North Carolina, like parts of the Chesapeake, had become a "nest of pyrates." Piratical goods had been found among the personal effects of the governor of North Carolina and several other local authorities. Blackbeard had seized so many ships in the Chesapeake that the governor of Virginia, Alexander Spotswood, complained to the lords proprietors of the colony about the nest of pirates, but they ignored his complaint.[63] While Blackbeard was on his way to North Carolina, he met with some misfortune; he ran the *Queen Anne's Revenge* ashore at Ocracoke Inlet, along with two of the four sloops that he had under his command. Hoping to take advantage of the governor of North Carolina, who was known to be friendly to pirates operating out of the Chesapeake and the Carolinas, Blackbeard and several of his men decided to seek the king's pardon to avoid the hangman's noose.[64] Spotswood, who didn't believe the sincerity of Blackbeard's surrender or the integrity of the North Carolina authorities, issued his own proclamation. In it, he forbade surrendered pirates to carry arms or assemble in numbers. Spotswood also argued that Blackbeard would return to his old trade the moment his money had been spent at the local brothels and taverns.

Spotswood had right to be concerned, because that's exactly what Blackbeard and his men did. Spotswood learned that they "went out at pleasure, committing robberys on this coast" and had "brought in a ship laden with sugar and cocoa." Blackbeard's men said that the ship had been lawfully plundered as a shipwreck, but they had no papers to prove this, so they set it on fire to prevent identification. When Spotswood found out that they had plundered several more vessels near his coastline, he "judged it high time to destroy that crew of villains" and to not allow them to gather any more strength in the valuable region of the Chesapeake.[65]

So, Spotswood put a plan into motion. He sent for the captains of His Majesty's men-of-war off the coast of Carolina and Virginia to communicate his plan, but the captains were concerned that their vessels would not be able to maneuver the shallow and difficult channels of the region. They also didn't have the authority to hire the sloops that could, so they would have had to pay out of their own pockets for them. Governor Spotswood eventually persuaded them, and after they promised to provide him with men, he took on the financial burden of refitting his own sloops and hiring two new sloops. In late December 1718, Spotswood's men embarked on their new mission. They quickly came upon Blackbeard on December 22; he was aboard a sloop with eight guns and men who were well fitted for a fight. When Blackbeard caught sight of them and realized that the king's men intended to board him, he chugged a bowl of liquor and shouted that he "drank damnation to anyone that should give or ask quarter" before firing his guns.

Twenty of the king's men were either killed or wounded, which gave Blackbeard the initial advantage. Blackbeard ordered that should he fall, his ship was to be blown up. He, along with several of his men, boarded the sloop, deftly wielding their cutlasses and shooting their pistols. Some witnesses reported that Blackbeard and his men filled the sloop with smoke

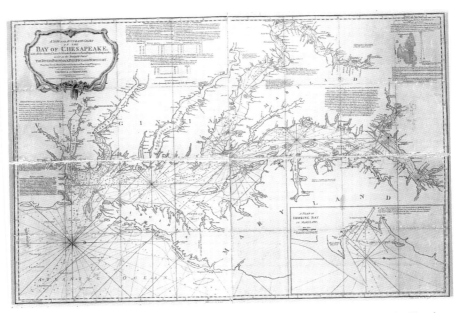

A new and accurate chart of the Bay of Chesapeake, with all the shoals, channels, islands, entrances, soundings and sailing marks, circa 1776. *Courtesy of the Library of Congress Geography and Map Division.*

through the use of powder and shot in small bottles. Once he was on board, Blackbeard shot at the lieutenant of the sloop, who fired back and wounded Blackbeard. The pair engaged their cutlasses in a dance to the death until the lieutenant's sword broke in half. As Blackbeard went to deal a fatal blow to the lieutenant, who was cocking his pistol, one of the lieutenant's men gave Blackbeard a "terrible wound in the neck and throat."[66]

Ultimately, Blackbeard and his crew killed eleven of the king's men and wounded twenty-three, but this would prove to be Blackbeard's last stand. He, along with nine of his crewmembers, were killed in the melee. Blackbeard himself fought with "great fury" until his body could no longer withstand the twenty-five wounds he had received—five of which were gunshot wounds. The lieutenant, who had cocked his pistol one last time, fired the fatal blow. Contrary to Blackbeard's orders, his ship was not blown up, as one of the hostages thwarted the man who was in charge of the powder. Thus, Blackbeard's reign of terror in the Chesapeake and beyond ended.

LEGENDS

There are countless rumors of pirates and buried treasure along the coasts between Charleston to Baltimore and beyond. Since most of these legends are mere speculation, is it possible that some of our own pirates are actually legend as well? Some loom large in our imaginations. For example, in 1746, five men were apprehended on Chincoteague Island. They claimed to be crewmembers of the Spanish privateersman Don Pedro but were actually believed to be escaped enslaved men from Pennsylvania. Before they were arrested, the men had entered Maryland's Sinepuxent Inlet in a rowboat. The men had only a sheep and a broken scythe among them. As they crawled through the inlet, they came across a sloop, killed one of its crewmen and injured the other. Using this new sloop, the men supposedly plundered their way south, increasing their arms, taking hostages and stealing supplies. But as they pulled into Chincoteague Inlet, they were apprehended after a brief gunfight. One of the men was killed, while the other four were convicted and executed. Although their names are lost to us, their story continues to resonate in the folklore of Chesapeake piracy. They now represent just how legendary pirates were at the time: even enslaved blacks, who had escaped their bondage, could take cues from pirate tales and turn to piracy themselves.

Perhaps the greatest rumor of buried treasure in the Chesapeake is that of Charles Wilson's loot. Legend has it that Wilson was a pirate with a hideout at Woody Knoll in Worcester County, Maryland, and on Assateague Island. But it was at Chincoteague that he reportedly buried his treasure, which was perhaps worth upward of $4 million in today's currency. In a letter that is said to have been written by Wilson, he said to his brother:

> There are three creeks lying 100 paces or more north of the second inlet above Chincoteague Island, Virginia, which is at the Southward end of the peninsula. At the head of the third creek, to the northward, is a bluff facing the Atlantic Ocean with three cedar trees growing on it, each about 1⅓ yards apart. Between the trees, I buried in ten iron-bound chests, bars of silver, gold, diamonds and jewels to the sum of 200,000 pounds sterling. Go to the Woody Knoll secretly and remove the treasure.

The letter reads more like a riddle than a map to buried treasure, but it hasn't stopped treasure seekers from hiking around the Chesapeake in an attempt to get their hands on Pirate Wilson's buried hoard. Will you be the lucky hunter who finds the treasure?

PART II

PATRIOTS AND LOYALISTS:
PIRATES OF THE REVOLUTION

1754-1783

*T*he moon shone brightly overhead as Captain Roache planned his next move. It was close to midnight on March 30, 1779, and the American Revolution had been underway for the better part of three years. Roache's crew was small, consisting of two white men and two black men, and armed to the teeth. They were cruising around Dames Quarter in Somerset County on the coast of Maryland when they noticed a schooner that was resting. Silently, the men sidled up to the schooner and caught its operators, Charles Hamilton and Athanasius Jarboe, off guard. Roache forced the men to hand over their weapons while he sent his lieutenant to search the hold. All the lieutenant could find was a bag of corn, a keg and ten gallons of brandy.

Roache and his men had no intention of harming the men or their schooner until Roache found a Continental flag on board. Roache and his men were Tories—or Loyalists—who had remained committed to King George III and Great Britain. They had been given orders from a colleague to destroy all Continental ships, but Roache was feeling merciful. Rather than kill the men, Roache demanded an oath of loyalty from Hamilton and Jarboe that they would never sail against the king again. In order to save their skins, the two men obliged, but as soon as they made it to shore, they reported an "act of piracy" to Colonel George Daishell. Apparently, these particular acts were quite frequent; Daishell wrote to the governor of Maryland regarding the incident and noted that, just the day before, he had been approached by a group of citizens asking him to stop the pirates.

He requested that he be granted the authority to raise a militia and several privateers who would man the coast and prevent such villainous rogues from disrupting peaceful trade in the bay.[67]

Much like this incident suggests, the American Revolution, which is often viewed through an "us versus them" lens in which the proud, patriotic American colonists rebelled against an oppressive and cruel king, was anything but. And when Americans think about privateers during the Revolution, they tend to imagine the thousands of individuals who volunteered their time, money, vessels and lives in support of the Continental navy and revolutionary cause. Certainly, these privateers were an important component in the war, but not everyone in the colonies was on the side of revolution. These Patriots contended, not only with the Royal Navy, but with the Loyalists among them who also operated as privateers for the British. Admiral Howe's 1777 invasion of the Chesapeake further fed Loyalist sentiment in the region, and in the fall of 1780, when British general Alexander Leslie arrived in the bay, the presence of 2,500 soldiers and the Royal Navy was enough to renew the spirit of any faltering Loyalist picaroons. Of course, these men were considered pirates by the Patriots, just as the actions of American privateers were considered piratical by the British. So, what role did these two groups play in the Chesapeake Bay, and how did they impact the outcome of the war?

Of the six colonies that hosted home bases for privateering missions, Maryland (Baltimore) and Virginia (Richmond) were home to two of the major ports. Nearly 1,700 letters of marque were issued to American privateers during the war, over 55,000 men answered the call and over 800 vessels were outfitted for these ventures. In Maryland alone, over 224 letters of marque were granted (although this number exceeds the number of actual ships that set forth from the state). There were 14 total letters granted in 1776, 33 in 1777, 42 in 1778, 49 in 1779, 61 in 1780 and 25 in 1781.[68] It's nearly impossible to determine the exact number of vessels that passed through the Chesapeake, because the changes in the vessels' names, rigging, ownership and the number of guns and crewmembers they carried affected their identification. Ships received 5 letters of marque, brigs received 31, brigantines received 27, schooners received 97 and sloops received 57. Records also list two boats, a barge and a polacre that received letters of marque.

The Baltimore clipper, a type of schooner, was a vessel that was particularly popular among privateers, and they first appeared during the American Revolution. The superior construction and sailing abilities of Baltimore

Baltimore Harbor printed and lithographed by Edward Weber & Co. *Courtesy of the Library of Congress Prints and Photographs Division.*

clippers were just a few of the reasons that Baltimore became such an important hub during the war.[69] Privateers were particularly crucial to the survival of the Chesapeake Bay. In terms of preserving themselves against enemy pirates, privateers and the Royal Navy, the Chesapeake found itself relatively defenseless. Maryland's state navy was all but nonexistent, save for two small schooners called the *Dolphin* and the *Platter*, as the rest had been auctioned off. And Virginia's forces were depleted, as they were attempting to defend the entirety of the bay. The Chesapeake Bay was a critical route for communications from Philadelphia to the southern colonies, and Loyalist privateers not only interrupted those communiques, but they also threw the financial stability of Continental forces into turmoil.

THE *BALTIMORE HERO*

The ink on the Declaration of Independence barely had time to dry before the Maryland privateering sloop the *Baltimore Hero* was commissioned.

The vessel was originally owned by Abraham Van Bibber, John Crockett and Thomas Ringgold of Baltimore, Maryland, and Robert T. Hooe of Alexandria, Virginia, and it put up a total bond of $5,000. The vessel was placed under the command of Thomas Waters, with William Jones as first mate, John Pine as second mate and John Sharp as third mate. All four men hailed from Baltimore. The vessel began as a fifty-ton ship with six cannons, six swivel guns and a crew of twenty-four men; it had permission from the Maryland Council of Safety to sail for Martinique in the French West Indies or some other foreign port. They first made for the neutral port of St. Eustatia in the Dutch West Indies, where Commander Waters refitted the *Baltimore Hero*. The crew then began running out of the port to seize prizes, which did a lot of damage to British shipping.[70]

Their first cruise proved to be modestly successful. A month after their departure from Baltimore, the men caught sight of a brig called the *May*— under the command of William Taylor—about three miles from Sandy Point on the island of St. Christopher's in the British West Indies. Per their instructions, the men viewed this to be a legally gained prize. However, according to depositions from the men who were on board *May*, the prize was taken in Dutch territorial waters and under the guns of the Dutch fort at St. Eustatius; this was also witnessed by the governor of the island. If these claims were true, they would have placed the prize outside the purview of the *Baltimore Hero*'s letter of marque. The *May* was en route from Dominica to St. Eustatius when it was captured. So, sensing the potential trouble this prize may have generated, Waters refused to give his true name and stated that he was Ezekiel John Dorsey. The potential trouble didn't stop Waters's men from bringing the *May* back to St. Eustatius, with the *Baltimore Hero* proudly flying the American colors, and bragging about their prize.[71] While the British lodged protest after protest to the governor of the Dutch island, Waters and his men moved on to seek additional prizes.

By March 1777, reports indicate that Waters had increased his power from six cannons to eight and had doubled the size of his crew to fifty men. It's unclear what happened with their prize from four months prior or what prizes the men took in the meantime. The crew's next recorded capture took place in August 1777, when Waters, who was using the name Halsey, took the *Catherine*, which was laden with rum and sugar, from Tobago. However, unfortunately for Waters and his men, the British "rose on them" and recaptured the *Catherine*. For unknown reasons—perhaps due to Waters's behavior—the *Baltimore Hero* was recommissioned in May 1779. This time, it was under the command of John Earle and his first mate, William Britton,

The Port of Baltimore in Maryland, circa 1718. This map shows fortifications, troop encampments and roads from "White Marsh," "Frederick Town" and "Spuriens." *Courtesy of the Library of Congress Geography and Map Division.*

who were both from Philadelphia. The new owners of the *Baltimore Hero* were Benjamin and John Crockett, John Sterett and others from Baltimore. They updated the ship from a sloop to a schooner that weighed eighty tons and had fourteen guns, six swivels and thirty-one crewmembers.[72]

In June 1779, the *Baltimore Hero* set sail for St. Eustatius. The ship was joined by the Maryland privateer brig called the *Lively*, commanded by James Belt; the *Lady Washington*, commanded by Joseph Greenway; and four pilot boats. When they were off the Rappahannock River in the Chesapeake Bay, near Virginia, they "fell in" with two enemy privateer ships that had twelve guns each and were leading two prizes. For two and a half hours, both Belt and Earle exchanged a hail of gunfire, and it seemed like they had "every prospect of taking them." But their efforts were thwarted when two more enemy brigs and enemy schooners intervened on behalf of their failing brethren. Deciding to make the best of a bad situation, Earle and Belt managed to recapture one of the prizes and sent it up the Rappahanock.

The *Baltimore Hero* came away with only three of its crewmembers slightly wounded, but its sails, rigging and hull were "much damaged." The *Lively* had two men who were mortally wounded, and the vessel was in equally poor shape. The British chased the *Baltimore Hero* up to Point-No-Point, north of the Potomac River in Maryland, before retreating. Earle and Belt made it to Annapolis to refit their vessels and had a plan to sail in a day or two with additional privateers in force. They needed more men "in case they should come across [the British] again, they will give them a very warm reception." The Maryland Council loaned some munitions to the *Baltimore Hero*, including 188 rounds of three-pound shot, and sent it on its way to St. Eustatius. In late October 1779, it was reported that the *Baltimore Hero* had arrived in Baltimore from St. Eustatius.[73]

JOHN GREENWOOD VERSUS JOSEPH WHELAND JR.

In the summer of 1781, John Greenwood was a second mate to a privateer with a letter of marque from Boston. While sailing in and around Baltimore, Greenwood found his captain to "be afraid of his own shadow"; so, rather than serve a coward, he planned to venture off on his own. Once he had enough money from his voyages, Greenwood convinced the ship's first mate, Myrick, to join him. The pair purchased a small forty-ton schooner to carry freight throughout the Chesapeake Bay. Their first venture proved successful enough, despite some minor difficulties. But the issues proved to be too much for Myrick to bear, and he sold his share of the schooner to a man from Fell's Point in Baltimore. At the same time that Cornwallis was seizing Yorktown, Greenwood was taking a freight of rigging down the Piankatank River. He managed to unload his goods and pick up oats that were bound for Baltimore. In addition to the oats, Greenwood took on seven new passengers who had considerable sums of money on them; they were all victualers and sold rum to the Continental army.[74]

On this trip, however, they didn't get far, because the wind and tide were unfavorable. So, the crew became obnoxiously drunk, and Greenwood sent them to sleep in the cabin while he kept watch on the vessel. When the tide turned, Greenwood pulled up anchor and headed out into the bay. He then called his partner to come take the helm while he took his turn to sleep. Unbeknownst to Greenwood, there were two British galleys lying in wait, just out of sight. Greenwood barely had time to close his eyes when he heard "a great noise on deck with swords and cutlasses." At first, he assumed that

Ships in a Stormy Sea, illustration from between the mid-seventeenth and early eighteenth century by Ludolf Backhuysen. Drawn with pen, brown ink and gray wash over traces of black chalk. *Courtesy of the Metropolitan Museum of Art.*

the crew was playing around, so he shouted at them to shut the hell up. But no sooner had the words left his lips than his hatchway was opened, and he was struck several times with the pommel of a sword. When he got to the deck, he saw no English flag flying; he assumed that these men were pirates. The captain's name was Joseph Wheland Jr.; he was a "tall, slim, gallows-looking fellow" wearing a gold-laced jacket. Wheland was offended at Greenwood's accusation of piracy.[75] He denied it and claimed that he held a good commission from the British to seize any vessels in the bay.[76]

Greenwood apologized, explaining that he thought the vessel was actually one of their own from Annapolis, "who would at times board and plunder even [his] own vessels." The majority of Greenwood's passengers were imprisoned aboard Wheland's galley, while Greenwood's partner was held on the smaller of the two galleys for "abusing" Wheland. Greenwood and several of Wheland's men, including a "mulatto" captain named George, were left on board Greenwood's schooner. Wheland's men tied the smaller galley to the schooner to be towed, and Greenwood was forced to join Wheland's plan: to sail up the Piankatank River and rob a Mr. Gwynn on Gwynn's Island. Gwynn's Island was where Greenwood had deposited his earlier freight, including a hogshead of rum. After Wheland and his men had robbed Gwynn, they caught sight of a drogher laden with tobacco and made chase, but they were unsuccessful in capturing this vessel, because the smaller galley they were towing slowed the crew down.

Greenwood had no intention of remaining imprisoned and forced to carry out depredations against his countrymen, so he concocted a plan, along with his fellow prisoners, to take the schooner back, as Wheland had only placed four men on board to manage it. First, they convinced Captain George that there was money hidden in the cabin. While he went to search for it, Greenwood called to one of the other men on deck, grabbed him by the collar, tripped him and threw him into the cabin. At the same time, Greenwood's partner seized a cutlass that the man at the helm had carelessly left on the stern-sheets and struck him down with it. The fourth and final man tried to strike Greenwood but missed and dropped his cutlass. Seeing no way to win the fight, the man jumped overboard and drowned. Greenwood and his men steered the vessel toward Baltimore seeking shelter.[77]

As Greenwood and his small crew made their way to Baltimore without provisions, both the smaller and larger galleys under Wheland's command chased them. The pirates fired shot after shot at Greenwood and his men, but they were "such bad marksmen" that they couldn't hit any of them. Greenwood described the pirates as "a set of gallows-marked rascals, fit for nothing but thieves; hellhounds and plunderers from inoffensive, unarmed people, they seemed to be without any kind of principle." He didn't believe they were operating as real privateers, because their objective was plunder. They didn't care what vessel they despoiled, be it loyal or otherwise; financial gain and "to acquire from others what they were, through mere laziness, unable to obtain for themselves" were their only objectives. The small galley fell behind, but Wheland continued chasing after the schooner.[78]

The wind was in the schooner's favor, however, and Greenwood and his men outsailed the galley. Wheland gave up the chase and made his way back to Gwynn's Island, where he deposited his own prisoners. While Wheland was there, he told the prisoners that, had he overtaken the schooner, he would have massacred the men who had retaken it. Greenwood fully believed that Wheland would have done just that. According to Greenwood, Wheland appeared to be "as great a villain as ever was unhung and all such characters the British seemed to encourage in their employ." After much difficulty, Greenwood and his men made it to Baltimore, but not before they were attacked by another pirate. Since the Chesapeake was, at that time, "infested by innumerable pickaroons, barges, gallies and small privateers," it was through sheer luck that they were able to, yet again, escape the villains. After his encounter with Wheland, Greenwood found that he'd had enough of sailing the bay and sold his share of the schooner.[79]

JOSEPH WHELAND JR.'S EARLY CAREER

As the previous account indicates, Joseph Wheland Jr. was perhaps the most notorious Loyalist picaroon. Wheland was active long before his encounter with Greenwood. His first Loyalist efforts began in 1776, when he carried goods up the Potomac River to Somerset County, hoping to trade with Lord Dunmore's fleet. His picaroon career, however, started that summer when he landed unopposed on Hopkins Island while commanding a small fleet. While there, Wheland and his men seized as many as sixty heads of cattle, two men and "everything else that was valuable."[80] Somerset County was an important location for Loyalist activity, but Wheland and his raiders launched a strike against the county, which threw local Patriot forces into mass confusion. It seems that, in some cases, Wheland's men operated out of personal vendetta rather than Loyalism. Wheland's attack on William Roberts, a wealthy farmer from the area, is one example of this. One of Wheland's associates took issue with Roberts and decided to seek revenge. Under the cloak of darkness, Wheland and his crew ensnared the man while he was asleep in bed, tied his hands and feet and took him as their prisoner. The men also stole a number of his enslaved men and women and a large amount of his personal property. High from their success, the men carried out another vendetta a few nights later when they burned a home on Nanticoke Point.

Wheland's attacks were unpredictable, and his depredations were vicious. With each new success, Wheland gained the support of other Loyalists throughout the bay. While he was hanging around Nanticoke Point, Wheland fell in among a group of other picaroons who had laid siege to the central region of the bay. He then seized the ship of a John White and outfitted it as his new vessel; he planned to add a total of sixteen guns to the ship in order to protect the Loyalists on the bay's islands from Patriot militiamen.

He continued his plundering along the Eastern Shore, and while he was cruising off the coast of Smith's Island, he caught sight of a boat laden with tar and planks. The boat had originally been bound for the Potomac River, but its crew had been frightened by the sight of Dunmore's fleet throughout the bay. However, they should have been more worried about the picaroons.[81] Before the vessel's captain, Mores Yell, had time to react, Wheland and his men descended on him. After boarding Yell's ship, Wheland first asked the man if he had seen Dunmore's fleet. When Yell replied that he had not only seen the fleet but had gone back to that island as a result, Wheland asked where he was from, where he was going and who he was working for. When Yell provided vague answers, Wheland asked whose side he was on, "The king or the Shirt Men [Americans]?" This time, Yell responded that he thought the Americans were in the right. It was then that Wheland revealed that he had a commission from Lord Dunmore to "take any vessel belonging to the rebels and to destroy such as he thought proper and carry the rest to the fleet." Wheland then demanded to see Yell's papers. Wheland took the papers, Yell's pocketbook that held about forty shillings in cash and "all the [clothes] belonging to this deponent that were in the vessel, except what he had on."

After Wheland had taken Yell's belongings, he took Yell hostage and placed him under the guard of a man named Marmaduke Mister. While Mister was keeping watch over Yell, he asked again who he supported, and Yell replied, "He was a friend to every person that behav'd well." But that answer wasn't good enough for Mister, and he asked again: king or country? Yell replied that he was born in America and had a "right to defend liberty." This offended Mister, who replied, "What these damn'd Rebels call liberty, I call slavery."[82]

Shortly after this exchange, Wheland told Yell about his seizure of White's boat and said that he needed Yell's mast to replace the one that had broken when he drove it aground. But before Wheland could repair his ship, he received an urgent dispatch from Lord Dunmore to come up the Potomac River and assist the fleet in getting water before it made its way to New York, Halifax and Martinique to fight the French. So, Wheland ordered his men to burn White's vessel and another that he couldn't maneuver over the sandbar. Wheland also released Yell, placed him on shore and returned some of his clothes.[83]

Later that summer, Wheland returned to his plundering ways. He, along with three of his men, took charge of another small schooner and sailed for the Hooper's Strait area. This time, however, a detachment of Patriots under the command of Major Fallin received intelligence of his schooner's presence in the area.[84] A detachment of Patriots set out immediately and caught up with Wheland. They seized the schooner and its cargo of one and a half hogsheads of rum, thirty bushels of salt, the sails and rigging of a sloop and a large quantity of iron, guns, swords and cartridges.[85] Wheland and his men faced charges of trading with Dunmore's fleet, piratically burning John White's sloop and a host of other crimes. The evidence against him—particularly the deposition of Mores Yell—was incriminating. He was found guilty of harboring strong Loyalist sentiments and of lusting for profit from piracy. Wheland was sentenced and imprisoned in Frederick County until he was able to offer full restitution to John White and made bond for good conduct. His men were also imprisoned until they were able to make bond. Over the next five years, Wheland tried to petition for his release, but to no avail. Wheland's imprisonment helped to temporarily reduce the number of picaroon depredations along the Eastern Shore, but he was soon back to avenge his name.[86]

MARMADUKE AND STEPHEN MISTER FILL THE VOID

While Wheland was in jail, other pirates tried to take his place. One such pirate was none other than Wheland's former shipmate Marmaduke Mister. Marmaduke enlisted the aid of his nephew Stephen Mister, and the two worked quite well together. Stephen plundered and Marmaduke sold the stolen goods at market. Unlike Wheland, who operated under the guise of being a Loyalist picaroon, the Misters were more concerned with gaining personal profit. In 1779, the men set up their base of operations on the Annemessex River near Somerset County, Maryland. Stephen Mister developed quite the reputation of his own while cruising the lower bay. In just one week, he managed to plunder a plantation, seize nearly a dozen vessels and effectively blockade the entire area of Nanticoke. The vessels he took were sent either to his uncle on Smith's Island or straight to the British.[87]

Tired of the depredations against their vessels, many within the bay demanded that the government put a stop to pirates like Stephen Mister and Carmine Smith. These were the same citizens who had approached Colonel George Daishell with their concerns. Daishell worked alongside the remaining Maryland schooners, the *Dolphin* and the *Platter*, to apprehend the picaroons. Daishell heard that many of the pirates had gone to the Pocomoke to hide their boats, so he moved quickly to secure the area. Daishell set up a temporary blockade in order to prevent the picaroons from seizing any more cargo and trading with the local inhabitants. Daishell's men searched for nearly two weeks to no avail; Mister and the other picaroons had eluded them. Although Daishell tried to set up a dragnet operation, Mister continued to evade him until the summer of 1780, when Patriot forces from Virginia apprehended him.[88]

WHELAND RETURNS

The summer of 1780 was not a good time for Patriot merchants and seafarers in the Chesapeake Bay region. From the Patuxent River in the north to Tangier Sound in the south, Tory picaroons raided with impunity. In July alone, it was reported that there were no fewer than twenty-five pirates actively raiding the bay and blocking the James River, and nearly a dozen Patriot vessels had fallen prey to the Loyalist picaroons. Because of this, most merchants found trading goods by water to be entirely too risky, but even the land had become a dangerous place, as raiders had taken to attacking inhabitants between the Potomac and Patuxent Rivers. By the fall of 1780, Tory pirates and privateers were in virtual control of the central bay, and their sights were set on the Eastern Shore.[89]

With Loyalist picaroons effectively blockading the region between the Potomac and Patuxent Rivers, a resurgence of Loyalist sentiment emerged. It was at this time that Joseph Wheland Jr. made his triumphant return. In the winter of 1780—after five years' imprisonment—two of Wheland's associates posted a £10,000 bond on Wheland's behalf. Although some report that Wheland promised to give up his Loyalist ways and join the Patriot cause, he was back to his old tricks shortly after his release. On August 31, 1781, Wheland seized the vessel of Captain Valentine Peyton from Stafford County, Virginia. A short while later, Wheland also plundered the ships of Captain Oakley Haddaway and William Barnes.[90] Unfortunately for his associates—who had each submitted £5,000 on his behalf—Wheland's bond was to be forfeited if he failed to appear before the council; and, of course, he was a no-show. Wheland continued plundering, unabated, and joined the countless others who made Patriot shipping nearly impossible well into the summer of 1781.

Wheland's next major hit occurred in July 1781, when he attacked a vessel in Hooper's Straight called the *Greyhound*. The ship was laden with "salt, peas, pork, bacon and some dry goods." Wheland held the *Greyhound*'s passengers prisoner for at least twenty-four hours and robbed them of all of their personal effects, including their money and watches. When the passengers were set ashore, one man remarked that he witnessed several other ships in the bay "fall into the fangs of the same vulture."[91] Wheland even acquired protégés, like Captain John McMullen, who commanded the picaroon barge called the *Restoration*. McMullen often worked alongside Wheland, and by the end of 1781, it no longer mattered to the picaroons whether their victims were Patriots or Tories. Unfortunately for McMulllen, Colonel Daishell had put together another flotilla to apprehend the picaroons, especially Wheland, who had humiliated Daishell by not becoming a Patriot as he had promised. The flotilla consisted of three barges, the *Intrepid*, the *Terrible* and the *Revenge*, which had been commissioned after the 1780 passage of the Bay Defense Act in Maryland. If the names of the vessels were any indication, the Patriots of the bay had clearly had enough of the picaroons and would do anything to stop them.

Within two days of setting off, the barges encountered a picaroon flotilla led by none other than Wheland, McMullen and another associate named Robinson. The picaroons scattered, and McMullen was easily taken. Robinson and Wheland fled, escaping the Patriot flotilla easily. However, the capture of McMullen was a great relief to inhabitants along the bay, especially when it was paired with the news that Wheland had left the bay. Ultimately, Wheland and Robinson made their way to the Carolinas, where they were apprehended, putting an end to Wheland's terror in the Chesapeake Bay.

BATTLE OF THE BARGES

After the passage of the Bay Defense Act in Maryland, a number of galleys and barges were commissioned in order to patrol the rivers, inlets and other waterways around the Chesapeake Bay. Some of these vessels were newly constructed, while others came from the local area or had been taken from the British. Not all of the commissioned ships belonged to the Maryland Navy; indeed, many in the bay—although they had been terrorized by the picaroons—saw privateering as a profitable option. Privateering also would have enabled them to keep their vessel once the war was over for personal use in trade. This mixed fleet of naval and privateer vessels faced the bloodiest engagement in the history of the Chesapeake Bay and the last naval engagement of the Revolutionary War.

Further financial assistance was needed to combat the Loyalist privateers, so in the spring of 1782, the Maryland Council passed the Act for the Protection of the Bay Trade. After the passage of the Act of Protection, even more help arrived; that fall, Commodore Zedekiah Whaley arrived in Baltimore with four ships that he had recaptured from Loyalist picaroons.[92] These ships were just what the local forces needed to prepare an offensive. That September, the Maryland Council charged Whaley with eradicating the picaroons in the Chesapeake Bay. Whaley was supposed to rendezvous with the French fleet and another American barge called the *Fearnaught*. But the council was not as strategically or logistically minded as Commodore Whaley, and they ordered him to set sail before he had time to store the amount of cargo he needed for the voyage.

Whaley ignored this first order, because he recognized that he was ill prepared and lacking the proper provisions to set sail again so soon. After Whaley's refusal, the council again ordered him to set sail. But the *Fearnaught* had still not arrived, so Whaley refused again. After the arrival of the *Fearnaught*, the council again ordered Whaley to leave, and this time, Whaley had no choice but to obey his orders. He did so without the French support that he needed, but luckily for him, the *Fearnaught* had arrived just in time. Whaley left Baltimore at the end of September 1782 with four heavily armed barges (the *Fearnaught*, the *Terrible*, the *Defence* and the flagship, the *Protector*) and one armed schooner (the *Flying Fish*). The schooner's primary job was to quickly carry supplies and messages to and from the barges.

The barges were not able to travel very quickly, but they did have one tactical advantage: their shallow draft made it easy for them to travel through the marshy inlets of the islands and tributaries in the bay. Whaley was joined by Captain Levin Spedden (the *Fearnaught*), Captain Robert Daishell (the *Terrible*), Captain Solomon Frazier (the *Defence*) and Captain Daniel Bryan (the *Flying Fish*). Colonel Whaley ultimately made Onancock Creek the base of the barges' operations, and he didn't have to wait long for his first encounter with British vessels. In mid-November, Whaley learned that no fewer than five British barges were near the mouth of the bay. On November 15, just off the coast of Gwynn's Island, Captain Frazier managed to intercept and capture one of the British barges, the *Jolly Tar*. Many of the prisoners from the barge were wanted picaroons; one of them had even been a lieutenant for Joseph Wheland. However, the second vessel that Whaley's men went after escaped from their grasp after a fifty-mile chase into the open ocean.[93]

A couple of weeks after this failed chase, Whaley's men got another chance at victory. Toward the end of November, Whaley and his men received intelligence that there was a small privateer near Watts Island with four prizes. As Whaley and his men got close to the island, they learned that that the privateers actually had seven vessels—six barges and one galley— and that they appeared to be on course for the Tangier Islands. Whaley believed that the picaroons were back with a vengeance. After weighing the risks, the consensus among Whaley's men was that they should go after the enemy vessels. But they realized they'd never take the ships before dark, so they decided to rendezvous at Watts Island. Once they arrived, the island was in the midst of a horrible storm.[94]

With time to strategize, Whaley decided that they would observe the enemy vessels during the following morning to determine whether a galley was really among them or if there were just six barges. If there was a galley, he decided that they would not engage the enemy, but if the barges were alone, he decided that they would attack. Not to be outnumbered by the enemy, Whaley sent a dispatch to the lieutenant of Accomack County telling him to send a fitted barge with volunteers and the barge that they'd taken earlier from the enemy. The lieutenant sent about twenty-five men and an eight-man barge called the *Langodoc*. Meanwhile, in order to secure as much information as he could about the enemy, Whaley dispatched Frazier and the *Defence* to Tangier Island. When Frazier arrived in the area, he saw no ships, so he landed on the shore near the home of a man named Crockett. Hoping to trick the Loyalists of the area, Frazier raised English colors and pretended to be a Tory. He began his ruse by first asking Crockett what he knew about the American ships. The man revealed that he knew very little, except that he'd seen five of them near Watts Island the day before. Crockett also said that six English barges had left his home that morning headed for Fox Island. Even more importantly, Crockett revealed that the barges intended to stop over at Cager's Straight for the night.[95]

Frazier returned to Whaley to inform him of what he'd learned from Crockett. After calling a council of the captains, the men decided that they were still confident in their ability to come away victorious from any conflict. They were joined by an additional twenty-five volunteers under the command of Colonel Cropper, a veteran of George Washington's army. The volunteers were divided up among the ships, and by 4:00 p.m. on November 29, the flotilla set off in search of the enemy. It took them many hours, but they finally neared Cager Straits around 4:00 a.m. the next morning. They received news that the enemy was, in fact, nearby, and after a couple of

The pirates' ruse luring a merchantman in the olden days, circa 1896. *The Library of Congress Prints and Photographs Division.*

hours of resting and rationing, they saw five of the barges at the entrance of the strait. Whaley gave the order to "make sail and give chase"; he didn't believe the barges would engage them directly, but if they did, he planned to create a line with his vessels in support of the flagship.[96]

As Whaley and his men neared the enemy barges at around 8:00 a.m., the enemy took in their sail and formed a line of five ships. The sixth barge sailed some distance to the right as if it was not intending to engage. Whaley and the others came within two hundered yards of the enemy barges, with the *Defence* and the *Terrible* a half mile ahead of the *Fearnaught*. The *Protector* was between them and the *Langodoc* and the *Flying Fish*, and they also took in sail and began to form their own line. At that point, the enemy picaroons began firing on Frazier, who returned in kind to the cheers of his comrades. Captain Spedden and Commodore Whaley joined Frazier in firing on the enemy barges. A melee ensued before Whaley realized that a fire had broken out near his mizzenmast. An eighteen-pound cartridge had been broken as it was pulled out of the chest and was spilling gunpowder on the deck of the *Protector*. Before the spilled gunpowder could be thoroughly dampened, it caught fire, which quickly spread to the ammunition chest and caused an explosion. Several of Whaley's men were killed instantly, while others jumped overboard to avoid the fire. A second explosion caused another fire, which killed more men and set several others alight. The Commodore's ship was thrown into absolute chaos.[97]

The enemy decided to take advantage of the situation, and two of their barges made moves to board the *Protector*, while the other three continued to fire on the *Defence*. In the meantime, Captain Frazier was informed that the men on the *Flying Fish* and *Langodoc* were "retreating as fast as they cou'd." The other three enemy barges made their moves to board the *Defence*. With all of the confusion, Frazier couldn't tell if there had been any signals for retreat or if he should continue. Soon, however, Frazier thought it prudent to get the hell out of Dodge, and Captain Spedden followed. At that point, the enemy was boarding Commodore Whaley's ship and the other barges were chasing after Frazier and Spedden. It was reported that Whaley and his men "fought with the greatest bravery" under a "shower of musket bullets, pikes, cold shot, cutlasses and iron stantials for eight or ten minutes" until they were overpowered and "obliged to surrender." Upon their surrender, Whaley's men were "most cruelly murdered and thrown overboard by the negroes." The losses sustained aboard the *Protector* were the highest of any naval engagement that involved the Maryland State Naval Forces during the entirety of the American Revolution. After several hours, the enemy picaroons gave up the chase of the other Patriot ships.[98]

Such a humiliating defeat was felt immediately in the surrounding area, particularly in Annapolis. According to Colonel Henry Dennis of Worcester County, the "situation of the people in this and Somerset Counties is truly distressing," because the enemy picaroons were "able to continue their depredations" unrelentingly. In the county, there were "neither arms nor ammunition were the Militia disposed to make use of them."[99] The situation in the Chesapeake was reaching a breaking point.

PART III

TRIALS AND TRIBULATIONS
OF A NEW NATION

THE WAR OF 1812

*T*he defeat of the British and the security of American independence was just the first of the new nation's concerns. At the top of America's agenda was the regulation of trade. How would the new nation's government regulate trade in a country that was founded on the evasion of trade laws? And how could it instill respect for the enforcement of trade laws among a populace that was accustomed to detesting them?[100] Many Americans—particularly those in the merchant class—had taken the "no taxation without representation" cry to literally mean no taxation under any circumstances, and they showed little respect for newly established customs services. So, the tradition of smuggling and illicit trading continued, not only in the familiar Atlantic ports, but also in new, distant markets.

Since smuggling usually involved evading the commercial laws of other nations, it was not much of a concern for U.S. collectors. But things became complicated for American traders and diplomats during the French Revolution and Napoleonic Wars. France, Great Britain and their respective allies were at war for more than twenty years, which presented the potential for immense risks and great rewards for American merchants who illicitly traded with both French and British privateers. American merchants didn't believe the trade to be illicit in nature; the United States had declared neutrality in 1793 and had therefore enabled its merchants to dominate the shipping of goods between warring European powers and their colonies.[101]

In 1805, other nations, particularly the British, began seizing American vessels as its neutral and contraband commerce became a point of

A Ship at Sea, illustration from between the mid-seventeenth and early eighteenth centuries by Ludolf Backhuysen. Drawn with pen, brown ink and gray wash over traces of black chalk. *Courtesy of the Metropolitan Museum of Art.*

contention. The British also announced that American merchants carrying goods from enemy ports had to show papers that stated the goods they were carrying were bound for the United States. If they could not produce the appropriate papers, the British would consider the goods to be contraband and therefore subject to seizure. American merchants incurred significant losses to British privateers, who the Americans believed were simply pirates. Americans were particularly galled at being relegated to a position that was no better than the one they had held as a colony. Even more concerning to Americans was the fact that the British were increasingly considering the crewmembers aboard their ships as human contraband. The British required the men aboard American ships to show documentation of their American citizenship; if they failed to produce this documentation, the men would be forcibly removed and impressed into the service of the Royal Navy. The British were suspicious of nearly every man's papers—they were easily forged—so many Americans fell victim to impressment.[102]

In 1807, President Thomas Jefferson instituted a series of embargos that he hoped would help to stave off war, and in 1809, when James Madison was elected president, he continued Jefferson's trade prohibitions. These embargos were meant to punish England and France for treating America's trade as illicit and violating American neutrality. But the implications of the embargos were ultimately worse for American merchants, as they criminalized much of their activities. After realizing that the restrictions were doing anything but preventing war—as the British continued to impress Americans into service for the Royal Navy—the United States officially declared war in June 1812. But the new nation was ill prepared to take on the most powerful navy in the world and ultimately relied very heavily on its privateers.

President Madison recognized the importance of privateers and personally signed each commission. Anyone who wanted a commission had to apply through the secretary of state and submit information about their ship and its crew. Letters of marque were extremely important; if a ship was captured by an enemy and able to produce an official letter of marque, it would be treated as a combatant vessel and its crewmembers would be treated as prisoners of war rather than hanged as ordinary pirates. The use of letters of marque was specifically mentioned in the declaration of war that was signed by President James Madison on June 18, 1812:

> *Be it enacted by the Senate and House of Representatives of the United States of America in Congress assembled, that war be and is hereby declared*

*to exist between the United Kingdom of Great Britain and Ireland and the
dependencies thereof, and the United States of America and their territories;
and the president of the United States is hereby authorized to use the whole
land and naval force of the United States, to carry the same into effect, and
to issue private armed vessels of the United States commissions or letters
of marque and general reprisal, in such form as he shall think proper, and
under the seal of the United States, against the vessels, goods, and effects of
the government of the said United Kingdom of Great Britain and Ireland,
and the subjects thereof.*[103]

The actions of these privateers contrasted quite sharply with the
performance of the U.S. military on land, and prominent American merchants
invested heavily in their success. Pirates, smugglers and privateers would play
celebrated roles in the war against the British, from the Battle of Baltimore
to the Battle of New Orleans, and they became folk heroes among the local
population.[104] In particular, the privateers from Baltimore were thorns in the
sides of the British. London newspapers frequently denounced Baltimore as
a "nest of pirates, which sent out its wasps to sting British commerce on every
sea." The British attack on Baltimore in September 1814 was, at least in part,
intended to punish the city for its connection to privateers.[105]

Impressment of American Seamen. A British officer looks over a group of American seamen on
the deck of a ship, circa 1810. *Courtesy of the Library of Congress Prints and Photographs Division.*

THOMAS KEMP, SHIPBUILDER EXTRAORDINAIRE

Between the end of the American Revolution in 1783 and 1797, over sixty thousand tons of commerce passed through Baltimore, and by 1800, the city was the third largest in the nation. As mentioned previously, Baltimore (Fell's Point, specifically) became renowned for producing fast, reliable ships called Baltimore schooners. Most, if not all, Baltimore schooners from this time period had one deck and two masts. Both the ability to reach high speeds and shallow drafts were critical components of the Baltimore schooner's design; these elements made them sleek and fast, but they also made them difficult to sail. A Baltimore schooner required a highly competent crew, which prevented the British from using captured ships against America. Between 1795 and 1835, a total of 421 schooners—each weighing, on average, 116 tons—were built in Fell's Point. They were all built by just eighty-three men, one of whom was a young man named Thomas Kemp. Kemp was a Quaker from the Eastern Shore who arrived in Baltimore in 1803; he became one of the most prolific shipbuilders in the Chesapeake Bay area. In December 1803, Kemp purchased property on the northeast corner of Market (now Broadway) and Lancaster Streets in Fell's Point. There, Kemp and his brother Joseph built a schooner called the *Thomas and Joseph*, but they mostly repaired the vessels of others.[106]

By July 1805, Kemp had saved enough money repairing vessels to establish his own shipyard on a property that was bounded by Fountain, Fleet and Washington Streets in Fell's Point. Kemp received all of his building material locally. His timber suppliers included Benjamin Bowen, Josiah Hall and Henry Hollbrook. He purchased spars from James Cordery and Joseph Robson, and he got his beams from Lloyd Johnson. For iron work, Kemp turned to Philip Cronmiller, and for copper spikes and rivets, he went to John S. Young. For finishing, Kemp got his rosin and pitch from John Stickney. Kemp employed about twenty-five men, most of whom were carpenters and caulkers, and he described the vessels they built as "round tuck privateer fashion schooners."[107] One of the first vessels built in the yard was a ninety-nine-ton schooner called the *Lynx*.

Kemp developed a reputation for building high-quality vessels that were known for their durability, reliability and speed. No other Baltimore shipwright at the time was as prolific or as accomplished. He built fifty-two total ships, and four of those belonged to the most successful privateers of the War of 1812; they were called the *Rossie*, the *Rolla*, the *Comet* and the *Chasseur*. Kemp often owned shares in the privateering ships from his yard, including the *Chasseur*, which was one of the fastest ships ever built. The *Chasseur* was granted a privateering commission in February 1813 under the command of William Wade; during its time under Wade, the *Chasseur* captured eleven enemy vessels. After the *Chasseur* daringly broke through the British blockade on Christmas Day in 1813, it docked in New York a few months later and was refitted. Some of its shares were sold to new investors, including its new captain, Thomas Boyle.[108] Boyle commanded the privateering ship called the *Comet* when Wade served as its second officer.

Captain Thomas Boyle and the *Comet*

Thomas Boyle was born in Marblehead, Massachusetts, but he considered Baltimore his home. His contemporaries saw him as one of the most successful privateers of his time, and he frequently challenged the British navy directly. He left such a trail of destruction behind him that by the time the War of 1812 ended, his contemporaries remarked that all of England knew his name. He aggravated the British "wherever he chanced to steer… carrying dismay and terror to British trade and commerce." His ship, the *Comet*, soon became an object of fear for civilians and the navy. Captain George Coggshell, one of Boyle's contemporaries and author of *The History of American Privateers*, described him as being a "dashing, brave man…. He evidently possessed many of the elements of a great man, for in him were blended the impetuous bravery of a Murat, with the prudence of a Wellington." Coggshell went on to say that if Boyle had been a commander in the United States Navy, "his fame and valor would have been lauded throughout our great republic; but as he only commanded a privateer, who speaks of him?"[109]

Boyle started his career at the tender age of ten and became the master of his own ship by his sixteenth birthday. During his time as a captain of privateers, he and his men captured between thirty and sixty ships. Boyle and his men first left Baltimore in July 1812 for a cruise that lasted for four months. The men managed to sail without hindrance from Bermuda to Brazil and back again. On this first venture, they managed to capture several small vessels, plunder their cargo and seize the ships as prizes. During one of their minor skirmishes, which only lasted for twelve minutes, Boyle's men boarded an enemy vessel called the *Henry*, a 400-ton ship from Hull that was commanded by James Dryden and had a crew of just twenty men. The ship

A view of the bombardment of Fort McHenry—near Baltimore—by the British fleet, circa 1819. *Courtesy of the Library of Congress Prints and Photographs Division.*

was sailing from St. Croix to London with 83 hogsheads, six tierces, seventy barrels of sugar, 19,160 pounds of Fustic, 3,640 pounds of lignum vitae and thirteen pipes of Madeira wine. Another ship, the *Hopewell*, was traveling to London from Surinam with thirteen guns, twenty-five men and a cargo of 710 hogsheads of sugar, 54 hogsheads of molasses, 111 bales of cotton, thirty-four casks of coffee, seventy-four bags of cocoa and an assortment of other goods. Some records estimate that the value of the *Hopewell*'s prizes was over $400,000. The *Comet* arrived back at Fort McHenry in October, after just eighty-three days of sailing. Boyle boasted that he had not lost a single man or been chased even once.[110]

After a month's refitting, the *Comet* set out for a second cruise in November 1812. This time, Boyle headed for Pernambuco in northeast Brazil, where he arrived in early January 1813. Boyle's second and third cruises were the ones that made him famous. First, during these cruises, Boyle completely outsailed several enemy vessels. Second, he easily defeated a Portuguese naval brig that was escorting three English ships bearing wheat to England. When Boyle spoke with the commander of the Portuguese chaperone, he remarked:

> [They] *were upon the high seas, the common highway of all nations, that* [the Portuguese] *had no right to protect them, that the high seas of right belonged to America as much as to any other power in the world, and that at all events (under those considerations) he was determined to exercise the authority he had, and capture those vessels if he could.*

After a brief cruise, Boyle and his men caught up to the three English vessels and seized each of them, one by one. Third, Boyle took more than twenty prizes. Boyle's venture was so successful that he became overburdened with prisoners and returned to Baltimore. He arrived in the city in mid-March 1813 and experienced no difficulties while passing through the British blockade around the Chesapeake Bay.[111]

THOMAS BOYLE AND THE *CHASSEUR*

In the spring of 1814, Boyle stepped down as the commander of the *Comet*, and in July 1814, he became the commander and part owner of the *Chasseur*. The *Chasseur* was considered one of the best privateering ships in the war; it had sixteen twelve-pound guns and carried over one hundred officers, seamen and marines. One of Boyle's contemporaries remarked that he was still "sometimes affected to chase the enemy's men-of-war of far superior force." An example of this can be seen in an incident where the *Chasseur* was surrounded by two frigates and two naval brigs. Despite being outnumbered, Boyle and his men slipped through and disappeared. For several months, the *Chasseur* sailed through the English Channel and along the coasts of Great Britain and Ireland. During this time, it captured eighteen prizes, including the brig *Eclipse*, which had fourteen guns; the *Commerce*, another brig with a copper hull; the schooner *Fox*; three additional brigs called the *Antelope*, the *Marquis of Cornwallis* and the *Atlantic*; and an eight-gun ship called the *James*.[112] Boyle gave a proclamation to one of the captains of these vessels and told him to post it at Lloyd's Coffee House in London:

> *I do, therefore, by virtue of the power and authority in me vested (possessing sufficient force), declare all the ports, harbors, bays, creeks, rivers, inlets, outlets, islands and sea coast of the United Kingdom of Great Britain and Ireland in a state of strict and rigorous blockade....And I do hereby caution and forbid the ships and vessels of all and every nation in amity and peace*

with the United States, from entering or attempting to enter, or from coming or attempting to come out of any of the said ports, harbors, bays, creeks, rivers, inlets, outlets, islands or sea coast under any pretense whatsoever! And that no person may plead ignorance of this, my proclamation, I have ordered the same to be made public in England.[113]

Boyle kept nine of his eighteen prizes (he sent the other nine back to the States), placed his men among them and held over 150 men prisoner. His depredations were so bothersome that the *Morning Chronicle* of London remarked, "The whole coast of Ireland, from Wexford round by Cape Clear to Carrickfergus, should have been, for above a month, under the unresisted domination of a few petty fly-by-nights from the blockaded ports of the United States is a grievance equally intolerable and disgraceful."[114] The success of the *Chasseur* and other American privateering ships severely affected British morale and caused their insurance rates to skyrocket. Some underwriters even refused to insure British ships and their cargoes for fear of their imminent loss.

Unlike his claims after his time on the *Comet*, Boyle could no longer claim that he hadn't suffered a single devastation after this cruise. While fighting with a frigate, it fired a twenty-four-pound shot that struck the *Chasseur*'s foremast and nearly destroyed it. Another shot "struck the gunwale of port No. 5, tore away all the sill and plank shear" and unseated the gun. The shot then crashed through the deck and wounded three men, including Henry Watson, who was "compelled to have his thigh amputated."[115] He sailed back to New York and arrived there in late October. Before Boyle could return to the water, he not only needed to refit his ship, but he also needed to make some alterations so that the vessel could be converted from brig to brigantine rigging whenever Boyle needed it to be. Boyle also replaced ten of his guns with carronades, which hit harder and were easier to load. By late December 1814, Boyle and the *Chasseur* were back in action. Although he exchanged shots with several vessels and escaped another, it's unclear whether or not he took any prizes during this particular run. The Treaty of Ghent, which technically ended the war, was signed on December 24, 1814, but news of the treaty hadn't yet reached Boyle (much like what happened to Andrew Jackson at the Battle of New Orleans), and in February 1815, he came across a new target: HMS *St. Lawrence*.

HMS *St. Lawrence* had actually been built in Philadelphia and was captured as a prize by the British in North Carolina. The vessel was equipped with thirteen guns and 76 men, while the *Chasseur* held fourteen guns and 102 men. Although they were fairly equally matched, Boyle mistook the vessel for a merchant ship, because he'd only seen three of its guns. Boyle attempted to close and board HMS *St. Lawrence*, but the *Chasseur* was sailing too fast to hit its mark. When the ships were just thirty feet apart, the men exchanged cannon fire. By the time the fighting ended, HMS *St. Lawrence*'s masts had been toppled, its hull and spars had been damaged and several men were wounded. After the skirmish, Boyle sent HMS *St. Lawrence* and its wounded crewmembers to Cuba. He described the vessel as having "a perfect wreck in her hull...[with] scarcely a sail or rope standing."[116] The damage to *Chasseur*, on the other hand, was mostly confined to its rigging and rails. In Boyle's account, he said, "At this time, both fires were very severe and destructive, and we found we have an [*sic*] heavy enemy to contend with....[I] saw the blood run freely from her scuppers." Reportedly, the British lost 15 men and had 19 more wounded, while Boyle only had 5 men killed and 19 wounded.[117]

In mid-March, a fellow American vessel from Boston passed along news of peace, so the *Chasseur* sailed up the Patapsco River, past Fort McHenry and into Baltimore. The *Niles' Register* dubbed the *Chasseur* the "pride of Baltimore." Today, a replica design of *The Pride of Baltimore II* still sails. On the *Chasseur*, Boyle captured twenty-three vessels, and the proceeds from the sale of those plundered cargoes totaled over $33,173.62. Boyle himself earned more than $30,000 from his cruises, both as a captain and as an owner of the *Comet* and the *Chasseur*.[118]

GEORGE R. ROBERTS

One of the men who served as a gunner on the *Chasseur* during its famous blockade of England in August 1814 was a free black man named George R. Roberts. Captain Boyle noted that Roberts "displayed the most intrepid courage," and he said that he was later "highly thought of by the citizen-soldiery" of Baltimore.[119] Roberts was even one of the few defenders of Baltimore who had his portrait taken by a photographer. Before serving on the *Chasseur*, Roberts was a member of Captain Richard Moon's privateering ship called the *Sarah Ann*. Some of the *Sarah Ann*'s investors included James Ramsey, the proprietor of the best chandlery and grocery in Fell's Point, and John Craig, another grocer who also owned several scows.

While Roberts was serving on the *Sarah Ann* in the Caribbean, the crew took a British ship that was carrying sugar and coffee. The battle only lasted for three hours, despite the fact that the *Sarah Ann* only had one gun to fire against the ten aboard the British *Elizabeth*. The crew of the *Sarah Ann* delivered the *Elizabeth* to Savannah, Georgia, before returning to sea, where in September 1812, they came across HMS *Statira*. Roberts was among six American seamen who were accused of being British subjects, taken prisoner and brought to Jamaica in irons when the *Sarah Ann* was captured. The men denied being British, and Captain Moon even remarked about Roberts: "I know him to be native born of the United States and of which he had every sufficient document, together with his free papers. He entered on board the *Sarah Ann* at Baltimore, where he is married."[120] Moon and his men retaliated, seized twelve British subjects and put them "into close confinement to be detained as hostages." Ultimately, the prisoners were exchanged. Afterward, in November 1812, Roberts arrived in Charleston, South Carolina, before eventually returning to Baltimore.[121]

It is unknown what Roberts's profession was after he served on the *Chasseur*, but he did become a local hero and was allowed to participate as one of the Old Defenders of Baltimore of 1814 during the parades that commemorated the anniversary for many years. According to one of the local newspapers upon Roberts's death in 1861:

> *Though laboring under the weight of so many years, his carriage was erect, and he never appeared on parade except in uniform, and it was one of his highest aspirations to still be considered one of the defenders of his native city should the necessity have arrived to take up arms in its defense. The deceased was one of the crew under the command of Captain Thomas Boyle, of this city, in the privateer* Chasseur, *when Captain Boyle declared the coast of Great Britain under blockade. He served during the war under several commanders, and generally at sea, and he had in the service many hair-breath [sic] escapes.*[122]

Roberts wasn't the only black Marylander to serve as a privateer in the War of 1812. He was joined by men like Percy Sullivan and Henry James of the *Tartar*; Charles Ball, who fought at the Battles of St. Leonard's Creek, Bladensburg and Baltimore with the U.S. Chesapeake Flotilla; and Gabriel Roulson and Caesar Wentworth, who served, respectively, as a landsman and a cook in the U.S. Chesapeake Flotilla in 1814. In addition to serving aboard a privateer ship, there were also countless mechanics who kept the vessels afloat, like George Anderson, Solomon Johnson, Elisha Rody and Jack Murray. Each man served in the Fell's Point shipyards as a naval mechanic.[123]

George Little: Twenty Years at Sea

Unfortunate circumstances brought George Little—born in Roxbury, Massachusetts—to a life of privateering during the War of 1812. He was on his sixth voyage when he arrived safely in Buenos Aires. It was there that he learned from his employers' creditors that his employer in Rio had gone bankrupt. The creditors seized the vessel and all the money and goods that were on board. When Little got back to Rio, he found that the condition of his employers was even worse than he'd anticipated. Two years' worth of his hard earnings were gone, except for $500. It was with this small sum that he took passage on a ship bound for Baltimore. He figured that it was best to get back to the United States after he heard word that war between the United States and England was imminent. Although the war had been declared two weeks before his arrival in the capes of Virginia, Little made it to Baltimore safely. There, he found "the most active preparations" in progress for war, including those of a number of privateers. He described the city's atmosphere by saying that he saw "everywhere the American flag" flying and "the most intense excitement prevailed throughout the city." Little realized quite quickly that if a man was "in any degree favorably disposed to the British," he would be subject to "the unpleasant affair of tarring and feathering."[124]

Hoping to find employment, Little made his way to Boston, where his family resided. His father, who had retired from the navy, tried to persuade Little to change his vocation. The war, he said, would destroy commerce and there was no alternative left for seamen but "the unhallowed pursuit of privateering." Although Little thought very seriously about entering into some business on shore, he realized that he had no idea what type of business to pursue and that his funds were quite limited. Fortunately for him, a wealthy relative offered Little the use of credit to set up a commission house, a business that executes the orders to buy and sell listed securities or commodity future contracts. A friend of Little's informed him that there were a lot of openings in Richmond, Virginia, for a commission house. However, when he reached Norfolk, Little realized that he had been deceived by his friend, who had no funds of his own and no way of assuming any. So, the establishment of a commission house was out of his reach and Little decided to try his luck in Norfolk, where "here too...all was bustle and excitement—drums beating, colors flying, soldiers enlisting, men shipping in the state's service and many privateers fitting out."[125]

Little was so moved by the spectacle that he joined the *George Washington* privateer ship as a first lieutenant. The *George Washington* was a 120-ton schooner with one twelve-pound gun, two long nine-pound guns and a complement of eighty men. The ship was said to be "as swift as anything that floated the ocean." Little was nervous about this new vocation. Sure, he said he was excited about the opportunity of making a fortune, but he was concerned about "getting [his] head knocked off" or "being thrown into prison for two or three years." But at that point, it was too late to back out. On the morning of July 20, 1812, the *George Washington*'s men weighed anchor and made sail down the river toward the bay. Little was impressed by the lieutenants and prize masters but felt that the captain was "a rough, uncouth sort of a chap, and appeared to...be fit for little else than fighting and plunder." The crew was no better, a "motley set...composed of all nations; they appeared to have been scraped together from the lowest dens of wretchedness and vice."[126]

The *George Washington*'s first objective was to cruise on the Spanish main and intercept English traders between the islands of the West Indies and mainland ports. The ship got as far as Lynnhaven Bay when it received intelligence from the pilot boat that a British frigate, the *Belvedere*, was cruising off the capes. This news caused a change in plans, and on the morning of July 2, the *George Washington* was underway from Lynnhaven Bay, which is about ten miles outside of Cape Henry lighthouse. There, they saw what appeared to be the *Belvedere*. After an hour skirmish, the men of the *George Washington* escaped without any damage, and since it was their first venture, they hailed it as a good omen—particularly because the frigate "was considered to be as fast as anything on our coast at the time." Because of this daring maneuver, the captain gained the confidence of the crew.

However, the *George Washington*'s next encounter was more embarrassing. As the vessel entered the Mona Passage—a strait that separates the islands of Hispaniola and Puerto Rico—it fell in with the *Black Joke*, another privateer from New York. Little and his men were unable to tell who the vessel belonged to in the thick fog, so the two ships collided and exchanged a few shots before they realized they were both hoisting American colors.

Given the weaknesses of the *Black Joke*, the two captains agreed to cruise together and to rendezvous in Carthage (Colombia) if they were separated. But the partnership didn't last long after they realized that for every knot the *Black Joke* sailed, the *George Washington* sailed two. So, they agreed to part ways and meet up again in Carthage.[127]

A couple of days later, the *George Washington* came across another ship and made chase. Once the *George Washington* was within range, the crew "let her have [their] midship gun" when the vessel turned and hoisted English colors. They realized that this would be a lawful prize, but the enemy ship's crew looked prepared to defend themselves, whatever the cost. And they did just that, cannonading the *George Washington*. At this point, Little himself witnessed the "daring intrepidity" of the captain of the enemy ship. Little said, "[While the vessel was] pouring a destructive fire into us, with the greatest coolness observed to the crew, 'That vessel, my lads, must be ours in ten minutes after I run this craft under her lee quarter.'" So, Little's men dropped on board the enemy vessel "like so many locusts," but not before "two of [his] lads were run through with boarding-pikes." While the enemy "made a brave defence," the men of the *George Washington* soon overpowered them through sheer superior numbers, and the captain of the brig was mortally wounded.

Just twenty minutes after the *George Washington* got alongside the British vessel, the crewmembers of the *George Washington* were waving the stars and stripes triumphantly. They lost only two men and had seven slightly wounded. This particular enemy ship had sailed from Jamaica and was laden with sugar, fruit and other commodities. It was a two-hundred-ton brig with six guns and only fifteen men. According to Little, "This affair very much disgusted me with privateering, especially when I saw so much loss of life, and beheld a band of ruthless desperadoes." He was repulsed by the "robbing and plundering of a few defenseless beings, who were pursuing both a lawful and peaceable calling." So, he resolved to quit his occupation at the earliest opportunity. He said he "could not help believing that no conscientious man could be engaged in privateering, and certainly there was no honor to be gained by it." But after repairing the minimal damage to the *George Washington*, its crewmembers steered for Carthage to fill up their water casks, replenish provisions and extend their cruise. The question on everyone's mind was whether Little would remain for the next round or not.[128]

Well, it turns out that Little wasn't quite ready to give up the cause. After a few days, the *George Washington* arrived at its destination and met up with the

Black Joke. As soon as the crew had filled up the water supplies, the captain of the *Black Joke* asked Little and the second lieutenant to cruise under both the American and the Carthaginian flag but to keep it a secret from the crew until they'd sailed from port. Both men rejected the captain's proposition, as it was "piracy to all intents and purposes, according to the law of nations." They also said that if he insisted, they would refuse to go out with the privateer. So, the captain gave up his nefarious idea. A few days later, they set sail in the company of the *Black Joke*. While together, the vessels captured several small British schooners. The crews divided the cargo and specie equally and placed all of the prisoners on one of the prizes with plenty of water and provisions. The remainder of the prizes were burned. The *George Washington* then parted company with *Black Joke* once more, as it needed to return to land for more water. But as they approached the shore—around 4:00 p.m.— they saw a small schooner ahead of them, and they weren't able to ascertain who it belonged to before darkness. The captain determined, then, to board the vessel under the cover of darkness.[129]

Although it was a dangerous idea, Little volunteered to lead the expedition, along with a sufficient number of men and two boats. The men were all strongly armed, their oars were muffled and grappling was available in each of their boats. The plan was to stay close together until they were in sight of the vessel. They then planned to board the bow, and Little's men agreed to board the quarter. They "proceeded in the most profound silence; nothing was heard, save now and then a slight splash of the oars in the water." As they neared the vessel, they noticed a light that was too high to be in the cabin windows. So, rather than give up the mission, the men decided to board simultaneously. Once they got on deck, Little ordered the men to proceed with great caution and to stay close together until "every hazard of the enterprise was ascertained." There was no opposition, and they found that "a large fire was in the caboose." The vessel was entirely deserted. Little surmised that the crew had caught sight of them earlier in the day. "Probably concluding that we should board them under cover of the night, they, no doubt, as soon as it was dark, took to their boats and deserted the vessel." They then set fire to the ship. The little cargo that remained on board was Jamaican sugar, rum and fruit.[130]

Little's men put out the fire and sailed the abandoned vessel back toward the *George Washington*, where the rest of their crew remained. They transferred any cargo that was valuable to the *George Washington* and put a prize master in charge of the new vessel. Little's men then made for shore to obtain water.[131] After a near-death experience, a harrowing escape from conflict with the local indigenous peoples and a blatant act of piracy against a Spanish schooner, Little and his second lieutenant had had enough. They demanded their discharge papers and their share of the prize money (which was $1,800 each). The men used those funds to purchase their own schooner, after which they acquired a commission to deliver freight and passengers to New Orleans and left their former privateers behind. Little, however, soon grew tired of life on land, and when he was asked to serve as a first officer on a Baltimore-built privateering vessel bound for Bordeaux, France, in October 1812, he agreed.[132]

Nothing of note transpired until Little reached the Maranilla Reef in the Florida Keys. On the morning of October 21, his ship fell in with an English frigate. They were fortunate to be windward of the English vessel, otherwise it would have "crippled [them], being within gun-shot." The English frigate gave chase all day, and "when night set in, under its cover, we altered our course and eluded the vigilance of the enemy." As they approached the Outer Banks of North Carolina, they again found themselves in trouble and caught between two English sloops. They made yet another narrow escape and were no doubt aided by the appearance of a storm. By mid-November they were within half a day's sail to Bordeaux when the wind "fell away calm." So, they were forced to wait. The next morning, they saw a ship and two brigs with English ensigns flying. It was impossible for the privateers to flee since the wind was dead calm and "resistance was entirely useless, for [they laid] at the mercy of their whole broadsides."[133]

At the time, the American colors were flying high on their vessel when they realized "to [their] great mortification, it must soon be hauled down in unresisting humility." At first, one of the vessels opened fire, and within twenty minutes, the English had boarded Little's ship and taken possession "of [the] valuable vessel and cargo." Fortunately for Little, he had had a premonition of imminent disaster and "had taken the precaution during the night to sew up in a flannel shirt all the money [he] had, consisting of seventeen doubloons, and then put it on." After gaining possession of the schooner and its cargo, the English robbed the men "of almost everything they could lay their hands upon." The American prisoners were then divided among the three ships, with the captain, Little and two other men put aboard the main ship. Then, the three English vessels dispersed. The ship on which Little was imprisoned was bound to cruise the coasts of Spain and Portugal. The captain and Little received good treatment from the British privateers and were assured that "the first licensed ship they fell in with, [they would] be released."[134]

But just three days after their capture, the British privateer fell in with an American schooner. The English felt that this would make another fine prize and made every preparation for action. As night drew near, the captain of the English vessel felt that the American schooner would not engage at night, so "every advantage was taken of the wind to get clear of her, but it was all in vain." By morning, the schooner was only a mile behind them. The captain of the English vessel ordered his prisoners back below deck when "a running fight commenced." Victory was decided in just thirty minutes; most of the English had deserted their quarters, and the British flag was hauled down. The English privateering ship became a prize for Paul Jones, a privateer of the *New York*, which had eighteen guns and 120 men. A scene of "plunder and robbery was perpetrated, by the privateer's crew." Clothing, cargo, provisions and coins were all taken "without any ceremony." The crew, Little said, "[was] a perfect set of desperadoes and outlaws, whom the officers could neither restrain nor command." Little and his own captain suffered the same fate as the English. They were held prisoner aboard the American vessel for some time before the American privateers eventually returned Little to Maryland.

JOSHUA BARNEY

Perhaps the most significant Baltimore privateer was Joshua Barney. Barney was born in Baltimore County, Maryland, and was a naval hero during the Revolutionary War. He joined the navy at the age of thirteen and was in command of his own ship by the time he was sixteen. Although he'd become a merchant after the American Revolutionary War, he still felt the patriotic call and volunteered to serve again in the summer of 1812. He was officially commissioned by President Madison himself to be a privateer aboard the *Rossie*. Barney immediately built upon his earlier naval successes. He frequently raided British ships on the open ocean and received significant press attention. The *Vermont Gazette* reported on the results of one of his raiding voyages in its August 31, 1812 issue:

> *Arrived at Boston the English brig* William, *from Bristol (England) for St. Johns, with 150 tons of coal, &c. a prize to the privateer* Rosie, *Commodore Barney, who had also captured and destroyed eleven other British vessels and captured the ship* Kitty, *from Glasgow, of 400 tons, and ordered her for the first port.*[135]

But despite his success as a privateer, Barney did not gain a lot of profit from his ventures. In 1813, using his reputation to his advantage, Barney approached the secretary of the navy, William Jones, with a request to create a special squadron—a small flotilla—to protect the vital waterways of the Chesapeake Bay. The Chesapeake had always been at the mercy of the Royal Navy, which practiced unrestricted warfare against the American men and women who lived in the Maryland and Virginia tidewater. At the time, the U.S. Navy was blockaded in the Elizabeth River by the British, which meant that those in the Chesapeake had to fend for themselves. Barney's plan came at a good time, as the British had authorized their commanders to "devastate and ravage the seaport towns" of the Chesapeake. So, Barney put his fleet together quickly once he had the authority to do so.

Each ship in the Chesapeake Flotilla—also known as Barney's Flying Squadron—was essentially a floating gun barge. They were all capable of maneuvering quickly and were designed to harass and distract the British warships in the Chesapeake Bay. By the end of April 1814, Barney was made a captain in the U.S. Navy, and in May 1814, the squadron, led by Barney's flagship—the sloop-rigged, self-propelled floating battery called USS *Scorpion*, which had two long guns and two carronades—headed down the Chesapeake to fulfill their mission. Because of their speed and maneuverability, the Chesapeake Flotilla also earned the nickname the "Mosquito Fleet." Each ship's crew consisted of veteran sailors, including enslaved and free African Americans like Charles Ball, Gabriel Roulson and Caesar Wentworth.[136]

Barney and his men had their first major engagement in June 1814. While cruising the Chesapeake, they encountered a twelve-gun schooner called HMS *St. Lawrence*, which was a former Baltimore privateer called the *Atlas*. They also saw the boats from two seventy-four-gun third rates called HMS *Dragon* and HMS *Albion* near St. Jerome Creek in Maryland. The flotilla made the decision to pursue the *St. Lawrence* and the other boats until they were able to reach the protection of the two third rates. The American flotilla then retreated into the Patuxent River, where the British quickly formed a blockade. Barney and his men were outnumbered seven to one, which forced the flotilla to retreat into St. Leonard's Creek. Two additional British frigates joined the mix: the thirty-eight-gun HMS *Loire* and the thirty-two-gun HMS *Narcissus*. They, along with an eighteen-gun sloop, HMS *Jasseur*, blockaded the mouth of the creek. But the creek was too shallow for their vessels to enter, which enabled the flotilla to hold steady. As the British sent their small boats to engage the flotilla, the flotilla outgunned them. Engagements between the British and the Chesapeake Flotilla continued for several days before the British, frustrated by the flotilla's ability to thwart their efforts, instituted a "campaign of terror." They destroyed "town and farm alike" and plundered and burned their way through Calverton, Huntingtown, Prince Frederick, Benedict and Lower Marlboro.[137]

The conflict continued for a few more weeks before Barney and his men were joined by U.S. Army colonel Decius Wadsworth and U.S. Marine Corps captain Samuel Miller. Feeling emboldened, Barney attempted to break the British blockade. Implementing simultaneous attacks from both land and sea allowed the flotilla to move out of St. Leonard's Creek and up to Benedict, Maryland. Barney did, however, lose two gunboats in the creek. Angered by their escape, the British entered the creek and burned the town of St. Leonard, Maryland, before moving up the Patuxent River to Benedict, Maryland. The secretary of the navy was concerned that the flotilla might fall into British hands and give them an advantage in the Chesapeake, so he ordered Barney to take the flotilla as far up the Patuxent as he could—to Queen Anne—and scuttle the entire flotilla should the British approach. Following orders, Barney left the barges near Pig Point with about one hundred men in case they needed to destroy the craft, and he took the rest of his men, who numbered over three hundred, to join General William Henry Winder in Prince George's County.[138]

There, they participated in the Battle of Bladensburg. In the meantime, the skeleton crew blew up all but one of the flotilla's vessels, which fell into British hands. But fortunately for Barney and General Winder, the destruction of more than sixteen ships blocked the channel and prevented the British from moving in farther. Barney and his men, alongside 120 U.S. Marines under the command of Captain Samuel Miller, took up a good defensive position on a hill outside of Bladensburg. But after four hours of intense hand-to-hand combat, they were overrun by the superior numbers of the British. Barney and his men were captured, but to everyone's astonishment, British general Ross was impressed with him and the military prowess of his flotilla crew, so he immediately pardoned them. During the battle, Barney received a bullet to his thigh that was lodged so deep it was never able to be extracted. Complications eventually set in, and he died in Pittsburgh, in 1818, while he was traveling to his new home in Kentucky.[139]

WAR'S END

The War of 1812 ended almost as quickly as it had begun, but not before the British could take Washington, D.C., and burn the White House, the Capitol building and a number of other important buildings. The British were simply retaliating for the earlier burning of the British government buildings in Canada by U.S. troops. The British didn't stay in Washington long, however, and they made their way to Fort McHenry in Baltimore Harbor. The harbor withstood a massive bombardment, which inspired Francis Scott Key to write a poem called "Defence of Fort M'Henry," which later formed the lyrics for "Star-Spangled Banner."

The tide again turned in the Americans' favor when, in September 1814, Thomas Macdonough's American naval force won a decisive victory at the Battle of Plattsburg Bay on Lake Champlain. This victory forced the British to abandon their invasion of the northeastern region of the United States and to retreat to Canada. This particular victory also led to the conclusion of the American-British peace negotiations in Belgium, and on December 24, 1814, the Treaty of Ghent was signed, and the war ended. But it took almost two months for news of the peace treaty to cross the Atlantic, and Americans heard about the Treaty of Ghent at the same time that they heard of the stunning victory of Andrew Jackson's forces at the Battle of New Orleans, which was fought a full two weeks *after* the war had concluded. It's clear, though, that the privateers of the Chesapeake Bay were important components of U.S. Naval strategy and played critical roles throughout the war.

PART IV

A NATION DIVIDED:
CONFEDERATE PIRATES,
RAIDERS AND PRIVATEERS

1860-1865

*I*n November 1860, Abraham Lincoln was elected as the sixteenth president of the United States. Almost immediately, the Southern states with enslaved populations began their secession proceedings. By the time Lincoln took office in March 1861, seven Southern states had seceded from the United States and formed the Confederate States of America (CSA). While Lincoln's election was the catalyst for secession, it was the Confederate firing on Fort Sumter in April 1861 that put a full-scale war into motion. In response to this attack, Lincoln issued a call for 42,000 volunteers to serve in the United States military for three years or until the war was over. Jefferson Davis, the president of the CSA, put out his own call and issued an invitation for Southerners to apply for letters of marque. Davis was not disappointed, as countless volunteers submitted applications; the Confederate Congress endorsed Davis's actions and supported the new Confederate privateers. These privateers served in support of the small Confederate States navy, which often had its own ships acting as commerce raiders and blockade runners. Bonds of $5,000 were required for privateering vessels that were manned by fewer than 150 men, and bonds of $10,000 were required for those with over 150 men. Davis required each letter of marque to be backed by a specific vessel; he would not issue blank commissions. Davis's commissions also made collecting prize money an easy affair. Lincoln responded to this by issuing his own proclamation, which said that "such [captured privateersmen would] be

U.S. revenue cutter *Aiken*, which was captured by the Confederate army and renamed *Petrel*, being sunk by U.S. frigate *St. Lawrence* in 1861. *Courtesy of the Library of Congress Prints and Photographs.*

held amenable to the laws of the United States for the prevention and punishment of piracy." This meant that any Confederate privateers who were captured would be hanged for piracy.[140]

The Chesapeake region found itself in a difficult situation at the outset of the American Civil War. In response to the situation at Fort Sumter, Virginia passed its own Ordinance of Secession on April 17, 1861. However, Maryland remained a member of the United States; the Chesapeake was a bay divided. Fort McHenry in Baltimore, Maryland, received a garrison of marines from the Washington Navy Yard as the Southern states began seceding in January. Baltimore was infamous for its violent politics and eventually earned the nickname "Mobtown." The city was teeming with support for the South, and many of its citizens called for Maryland's secession. Baltimore was the largest city on the Chesapeake, and it was truly a Southern city on the regional edge. It had hosted two Democratic National Conventions when the Democratic Party split into Northern and Southern factions. It also played host to the Constitutional Union Party, a short-lived mishmash of former Whigs and Know-Nothings. By 1861, Maryland's population was split, which was most distinctly felt in Baltimore.

An image of a sally port in Fort Monroe, Virginia, that shows Union guards among a group of men at the entrance to the fort in 1864. *Courtesy of the Library of Congress Prints and Photographs Division.*

The enslaved population in the state had declined to 87,000, while its free black population had risen to 84,000. And in Baltimore specifically, the number of enslaved peoples had dropped from 6,000 to 2,000 since 1830, while the free black population had risen to 25,000.[141]

Geographically and politically, Baltimore was on a fault line, and its business interests (its growing railroad and thriving shipping lines) straddled the divide between North and South. The city was also strategically located. Baltimore was the largest rail center near Washington, D.C., and Maryland itself surrounded the nation's capital on three sides. So, not only was Maryland itself an important chess piece, but its bay was as well. According to historian Eric Mills, the bay "was of immeasurable worth, an ultimate

FORT M^c HENRY, BALTIMORE, M^D

W.W. MORRIS, Col. 2^d Artillery, Com. of the Fort

Gen. J. A. DIX, Com. in Chief of this Dep^t.

S.M. ALFORD, Col. 3^d N.Y.V.

Fort McHenry in Baltimore, Maryland, circa 1861. *Courtesy of the Library of Congress Prints and Photographs Division.*

determinant of outcome, for whichever side could control her." The United States capital is just up the Potomac River from Baltimore, while the Confederate capital of Richmond is over one hundred miles up the James River. Whoever dominated the Chesapeake's waterways had the advantage of dictating the direction of the war.

At the outset of war, the U.S. Navy had forty-two commissioned vessels at its disposal. Yet most were already serving in foreign stations. The secretary of the navy, Gideon Wells, recalled all but three of these ships. Two of them, the *Pocahontas* and the *Cumberland*, were ordered to Fort Monroe—also known as the Gibraltar of the Chesapeake—in the Chesapeake Bay. They were there to protect the fort, which was connected to the Old Point Comfort mainland by a narrow strip of land. The fort looked over the lower part of the bay and controlled the confluence of the Nansemond, Elizabeth and James Rivers at the strategically vital deep-water channel and harbor of Hampton Roads.[142] Additionally, the Chesapeake housed the Washington Navy Yard and the impressive Norfolk Navy Yard. The Norfolk yard itself was worth $9,780,000 and was "a naval treasure trove in hostile territory." With Virginia's secession, the Norfolk yard was firmly in Confederate hands. Just a few days before Virginia seceded, a massive secession rally had been held in Baltimore, and a few days before that, a barque called the *Fanny*

Crenshaw had flown the palmetto flag of rebellion from the mizzen topmast. This act nearly sparked a waterfront riot. On April 18—the day after Virginia seceded—unknown individuals raised the secessionist flag on Federal hill to taunt troops at Fort McHenry.[143]

It truly was a battle for the Chesapeake, and Confederate privateers played an important role in the fight for this vital waterway.

John Taylor Wood and His Raiders

On August 12, 1863, John Taylor Wood led eleven officers and seventy-one men on four wheel-mounted raiding boats to raid the Chesapeake. Wood was a veteran of the Battle of Hampton Roads, one of the defenders of Drewry's Bluff on the James River and the nephew of Confederate president Jefferson Davis, whom he served as his naval aide. His exploits earned him the dual rank of captain in the Confederate States navy and colonel in the cavalry. Impressed, Davis charged Wood's men with taking something more valuable than a commercial ship; their goal was to seize a U.S. gunboat and wreak havoc with it. Just a few nights after receiving their mission, Wood and his men went on their first foray, rowing down the Piankatank to the bay. When they reached the bay, Wood's men only saw two unboardable gunboats, so they retired upriver and camped until they were able to try again. The next morning, they had a second chance, but their run-in with a U.S. boat patrol was less than successful. So, they raced to their wagons up the Piankatank, where they took their boats overland to the Rappahannock River. By August 19, Drewry and his men put in at Meachums Creek, just ten miles up the river from the bay. There, they found the Potomac Flotilla, which was made up of the *Currituck*, the *Reliance* and the *Satellite*.

According to a reporter from the *Richmond Dispatch*, who was along for Wood's raid, "One or all of these we were determined to have."[144] As the sun began to set, the four raiding boats entered the Rappahannock, and by nightfall, Wood had called all the boats together and given instructions for their attack. But there was no attack that night nor the next. It wasn't until August 22 that their prayers were answered. A dark change in the weather turned out to be most fortuitous for Wood's men. As lightning lit up the dark sky, Wood and his men saw two of the gunboats "pitching and rolling at anchor in the bay off Windmill Point." These swaying ships were the *Satellite* and the *Reliance*; they were so close to each other that they forced Wood and his men to board both ships at the same time. The men divided themselves in half and had two raiding boats for every gunboat. Wood's men also wore white armbands to help differentiate themselves from their enemies and to keep them from killing each other. According to one eyewitness, there were seven men at watch on board the *Satellite*, and all of them were easily overpowered despite putting up some resistance. The eyewitness himself fired seven shots before realizing that the ship was taken, and he jumped overboard to save himself.[145] The eyewitness also recounted how, prior to the attack, three men had come aboard to sell chickens, but he suspected that these men were really on a reconnaissance mission and had found where the ammunition stores and small arms were (these were the first things seized when Wood's men boarded the gunboat).

With two gunboats now in their possession, Wood and his men set their sights on catching the third gunboat, the *Currituck*. But after sailing in rocky waters for several hours, the *Currituck* was nowhere to be found, so Wood ordered his men to drop anchor in Grays Point the next morning. While they were anchored, Wood's men caught sight of three sails out on the bay, so they raised the U.S. flag and went after the ship. Wood successfully used the *Satellite* to capture each of these vessels. The first was a schooner out of Baltimore called the *Golden Rod*, and it was caught off Gwynns Island. The schooner was bound for Maine with a load of coal, which the *Satellite* desperately needed. Wood's men carried the *Golden Rod* up the Chesapeake and caught the other two ships off of the mouth of the Rappahannock River. The vessels, which were called the *Two Brothers* and the *Coquette*, were both from Philadelphia and were both laden with anchors and chains. Wood and his men towed all three ships upriver and coaled up the *Satellite* before going back down toward the bay to find the *Currituck*. However, the *Currituck* was well aware of the fates of both the *Satellite* and the *Reliance*; it had already made its way to the safety of Fort Monroe, where it was able to recruit reinforcements.

The tide turned against Wood and his men as three gunboats caught sight of them. Although Wood wanted to get into open water before the gunboats could get any closer, the weather prevented their vessel from doing so. Instead, Wood determined that they would head upriver as a storm opened over them. At daybreak, Wood's men plundered the coal schooner and burned it, as it was of no use to them anymore. At that time, both the *Satellite* and the *Reliance* were fully refueled and making their way toward Port Royal. The raiders were greeted warmly, as the Forty-Seventh and Forty-Eighth Alabama Regiments were stationed in town, but the men barely had

THE PIRATE "ALABAMA."

JOHN BULL (*furious.*) "Hallo! there, SEMMES; that's *my* Property. Fair play, you Rascal! If I'd suspected this, you'd never have *got out of Liverpool!*"

[Most of the property destroyed by the Pirate Semmes on board the vessels he has seized was insured in England, and the loss will consequently fall on Englishmen."—*Daily Paper.*]

The Pirate "Alabama," an anti–Confederate States of America political cartoon from *Harper's Weekly* that shows the anger of the English over the loss of the British-insured property that was destroyed by the Confederate ship in 1862. *Library of Congress Prints and Photographs Division.*

time to rest before U.S. forces reached King George Courthouse, which was just fifteen miles away.

Once U.S. naval forces reached Wood's ships, both vessels received heavy artillery fire and started to sink. Wood and his men stripped their prize vessels of their cannons, engines, anchors, chains and "everything of value" they could before they abandoned ship. They took their plunder to the railroad station at Milford Landing and returned to Richmond. Wood's foray in the Chesapeake was over. He was heading for the waters of the Carolinas by the beginning of 1854, but the void left by the departure of the "curse of the Potomac Flotilla" was easily filled by other like-minded commerce raiders.[146]

JOHN YATES BEALL AND BEALL'S PARTY

John Yates Beall's official military career was a short-lived one. While leading a cavalry charge at the Battle of Falling Waters in 1861, Beall was shot in the chest and deemed unfit for active duty. But his Confederate sympathies would not let him stand by while his compatriots fought against the so-called tyranny of the United States. Inspired by the actions of others, Beall believed he could be useful as the commander of a privateering ship, seizing U.S. vessels on the Great Lakes. Although Confederate authorities were interested in his privateering scheme, his chosen location was of concern; his activities could have endangered the South's relationship with Great Britain, which remained neutral during the conflict. They did, however, commission Beall as acting master in the Confederate States Navy (CSN), but he was not given a command. So, Beall set his sights on a new location: the Potomac River and the broader Chesapeake Bay region. The CSN said that if Beall could supply men and secure his own boats, they would provide the equipment he needed for privateering in the Chesapeake. Like all other privateers, the pay for Beall's men would be the U.S. prize ships that they seized on their voyages.

So, Beall and ten intrepid men set off in the footsteps of giants like John Taylor Wood.[147] They left Richmond in April 1863 and made their way to Mathews Courthouse. In their first month of operations, Beall and his men saw very little success. Their only engagement was with a camp of "contrabands" who were just ten miles from Fort Monroe; Beall and his men killed one contraband, captured another one and caused the rest to take flight. Afterward, Beall's party had more weapons, and his men were better equipped to launch larger attacks. In July, Beall commenced operations in the Chesapeake with open boats. Soon after reaching Mathews County, he caught sight of a U.S. steamer called the *George W. Rodgers*, and he made plans to capture it. But his squad arrived twenty minutes *after* the vessel had already departed, so he moved on to plan B: he cut the telegraph line between Fort Monroe and Washington. He sent a small piece of the line to the Confederate secretary of the navy as proof of his success.[148]

In August 1863, Beall and his party again set sail from Mathews County and crossed the Chesapeake Bay to make their way toward Smith's Island. There, they intended to destroy the Cape Charles Lighthouse. Beall and his men arrived at Smith's Island around 10:00 a.m. While hiding his crew, Beall and one of his men approached the lighthouse and the Northern sympathizer who kept it. Despite the man's Northern sympathies, Beall was able to charm him and learn all the "wonders and treasures" of the lighthouse before he called his men to rush the building. They immediately set about destroying "all the machinery, appurtenances and fixtures, and brought off three hundred gallons of oil, [which was], at that time, of great value in Richmond." Beall then threatened the lighthouse tenant and told him not to leave the island for at least twenty-four hours.[149]

As the news of Beall's exploits grew, so did the size of his crew. When he set out in September—again from Mathews—Beall's party numbered eighteen men. According to one of his new recruits, while the crew was in Mathews, they were treated very hospitably despite the very real danger that accompanied being friendly to the "notorious Beall and his party of pirates." The men were divided evenly between two boats; the *Swan* was painted white and commanded by Beall himself, while the *Raven* was black and led by Beall's second-in-command, Edward McGuire.[150] The ships sailed easily across the Chesapeake; they were able to reach Devil's Ditch by the night of September 18 and Northampton County the next afternoon. On the night of September 19, Beall's men passed by Smith's Island Lighthouse again, but this time, it was heavily defended by a new three-gun battery that had been erected in response to Beall's earlier attack. Fortunately for the men, Beall had other plans and bypassed the island. The men instead proceeded to Raccoon Island near Cape Charles, where they found a U.S. sloop called the *Mary Anne* and two fishing boats. Beall and his party seized all three vessels. Since his men were a little "fish hungry," Beall allowed the men to take as much fishing tackle as their hearts desired, and they spent the remainder of the day fishing in the sand shoals near Cobb's island.[151]

For the next couple of days, the men sailed out into the Atlantic and found themselves caught up in a blustering storm. On the night of September 21, they found a large schooner anchored at Wachapreague Inlet, which Captain Beall intended to seize. Beall's plan was for the men of the *Swan* to board the schooner on its port side while the men of the *Raven* attacked it from its starboard side. However, the weather proved to be uncooperative during their attempt; heavy winds and thunderous waves forced the *Raven* to crash against the schooner, which broke its own tiller and threw McGuire headfirst into the ocean. Fortunately for McGuire, he managed to get himself back on the boat before he drowned. The rapid current carried the *Raven* around the bow of the schooner and threw it into the *Swan*, which forced all the men to board the schooner from the port side. According to one of Beall's men, the "night was so dark and stormy that not a soul was found on deck." So, they made for the cabins.[152]

At the time that Beall's men boarded the ship, they had no idea what kind of vessel they were dealing with. Was it a warship? Was it a merchant vessel? How heavily manned and armed was it? Fortunately for them, it turned out to be a "handsome" merchant schooner called the *Alliance* that was laden with around $18,000 worth of goods bound for South Carolina. Beall and his party easily seized the ship, since no one on board put up much of a fight. Beall then ordered for samples of everything to be brought up to the deck, and his men "had a veritable feast of good things," as the ship was filled with "everything to eat, drink [and] smoke." After their feast, Beall's men returned to the *Swan* and the *Raven*, leaving only a guard aboard the *Alliance*. They captured three more ships: the *Houseman*, the *Samuel Pearsall* and the *Alexander*. After capturing a ship, Beall's men would strip it of all its valuables, including its nautical instruments, "which the Confederacy was badly in need [of]." They would then scuttle it and force it into the Atlantic Ocean.

Beall then made the decision to bring the *Alliance* and all the valuable cargo his men had seized to Mathews County in order to deliver it to the Southern cause. But as they made their way into the mouth of the Piankatank River, they were chased by a U.S. gunboat, and in the confusion, the pilot of the *Alliance* ran it aground. The gunboat continued to lay waste to the vessel as Beall's party unloaded as much of the cargo as they could before setting fire to the ship and heading ashore. Once they were on land, Beall's men took several wagons full of the cargo to Richmond.[153] Before Beall's crew could move on to their next venture, they were nearly captured by a large relief guard of U.S. troops, but they hid just five feet from the road in a ditch and managed to go unseen. The men then made camp at Dragon Swamp for several days before they learned that a large force of U.S. infantrymen, cavalrymen and artillerymen had returned to Fort Monroe aboard a fleet of gunboats. This meant that the coast was clear, and they could move on. After their departure, Beall was informed that U.S. troops had thoroughly searched for them and were deeply angered at the citizens of the Chesapeake region for aiding him and his men.

A squadron of U.S. cavalry was sent to the home of Sands Smith, one of the citizens who routinely invited Beall and his party into his home; Smith had even become a dear friend of Beall's. Some members of the cavalry insulted Mr. Smith, and he was so enraged that he grabbed his double-barreled shotgun and killed the first man who insulted him. Before he could reload his gun to shoot the next man, several of the cavalrymen assaulted him with their sabres; this attack injured him but not gravely. The cavalrymen then bound

Mr. Smith and tied him to the seat of a buggy, reserving punishment until after he could be tried before the entire command. Mr. Smith's daughters begged to see their father, but they were ruthlessly pushed aside. Mr. Smith was taken between Colonel Tabb's and Mathews Courthouse, where he was hanged by the roadside, his body riddled with bullets. When Beall received news of his friend's heinous treatment and death, he was overwhelmed with anger and grief. After this incident, Beall became more anxious than ever to cause injury to the United States. This mindset would be his downfall.[154]

In November, the *Raven* and the *Swan* once again crossed the Chesapeake Bay. Beall's men captured a schooner in which they planned to hide until nightfall, when they planned to capture a gunboat that was anchored near Chesconessex in Accomack County. Captain Beall, however, determined that it was best for them to hide in the *Raven* and the *Swan*, since they were finer ships than the schooners that they had seized. Beall was also afraid that the schooners would attract attention in the heavily fished area. So, he ordered several of his men to carry the ships out of sight, others to stay on board and keep watch and the rest to return to the schooner. They did as

A lithograph by Nathaniel Currier that shows American privateer *General Armstrong*, captained by Sam C. Reid, firing on British boats sent from HBM *Carnation* to capture it, circa 1838. *Courtesy of the Library of Congress Prints and Photographs Division.*

they were told. The men who kept watch on the *Swan* and the *Raven* didn't realize the mistake they'd made in their choice of location until the next morning, when what they thought was a secluded spot turned out to be quite visible. However, the men determined that it would have been more dangerous to find another inlet, so they remained where they were. Later that afternoon, they were approached by a fisherman who inquired about their identities. After they lied and stated that they were a hunting party from Baltimore, the man went on his way. Beall's men—who figured that the man had sailed for the hundreds of other fishing vessels near the mouth of the inlet—believed they'd just had a narrow escape, but luck was not on their side. The fisherman went straight to the gunboat that Beall was hoping to seize and revealed the Confederates' location.[155]

At around 5:00 p.m., the men aboard the *Swan* and the *Raven* saw two boats moving toward the mouth of the inlet. The vessels were two large barges with well-armed U.S. troops and "guns cocked and ready to fire upon [them]." Beall's men were ordered to surrender and reveal whose command they were under. The men immediately revealed that they were part of Beall's party, so the U.S. troops arrested all of them and towed the *Swan* and the *Raven* behind their gunboat. Since Captain Beall was aboard one of the schooners, he should have been able to escape, but he went to see what had become of the detachment he'd sent out and was surrounded and captured.

Beall's men were told that they would be treated and tried as pirates. After a short time, they were taken to Drummondtown jail, where they were held overnight before they were brought back on board the gunboat and taken farther up the bay. Captain Beall and his men were all placed in a large cabin on the main deck, which was guarded only by two sentinels. Beall came up with a plan for their escape, but a majority of his men sensed that this was a trap and refused to participate. It turned out that they were right: a full company of infantrymen remained on the upper deck and waited for Beall and his men to rush out so "that they might shoot down every man and thereby have done with Captain Beall and his party without any trouble of trial." The men were ultimately brought to Fort McHenry, Baltimore, where Beall remained until he was exchanged in May 1864.[156]

Beall immediately set about organizing another party of men with the hopes of capturing Johnson's Island in Ohio, where a large number of Confederate officers were being held prisoner. But the Confederate secretary of war, James Seddon, doubted that Beall could enlist a sufficient number of men for the dangerous mission. Beall, however, did manage to gather together a small group of volunteers, and in September 1864, they set sail for Johnson's Island. Along the way, they captured a ship called the *Philo Parsons* off Kelleys Island, and they captured the *Island Queen*, which they later scuttled. Beall's crew also planned to capture the U.S. gunboat *Michigan*, but unfortunately for Beall, his crew was concerned with the enormity of this task and refused to proceed further without outside assistance. Beall reluctantly agreed to forego the *Michigan*, and they sailed back toward Canada, where they scuttled the *Philo Parsons* and separated.

Nearly all of Beall's men escaped arrest, and Beall himself gave up his privateering plans. Instead, he decided to free some captured Confederate officers by derailing a passenger train. It was during this mission that Beall's luck finally ran out. He and a companion named George S. Anderson were arrested in Niagara, New York, in December 1864, and they were charged with irregular warfare (piracy) and spying. Anderson agreed to testify against Beall in return for leniency. Beall's trial began in January 1865, and by February, he was found guilty and sentenced to death. All efforts to spare his life were done in vain. On February 24, 1865, Beall was executed.[157]

THADDEUS FITZHUGH

Thaddeus Fitzhugh was captain of the Fifth Virginia Cavalry. He seemed to be the most unlikely of all the Civil War commerce raiders, but he worked quite successfully in that position. In March 1864, he led a very prosperous sacking of Cherrystone in Northampton County, Virginia; there, he captured the entire cavalry guard, including their horses, arms and a large supply of subsistence stores. These stores included "army bread, six hundred barrels of pork and bacon…flour, rice, molasses, beans, sugar, coffee," nine army coats and several army cooking stoves. Afterward, Fitzhugh and his men captured two U.S. steamers called the *Iolas* and the *Titan*, along with a large schooner.[158] Fitzhugh decided to sink the schooner, bond the *Iolas* and keep the *Titan*, which he carried safely across the bay and into the Piankatank River. He also cut the town's submarine telegraph line, destroyed its machinery and captured the operator of the telegraph line and paroled all the town's prisoners—and he accomplished all of this with just thirteen men.[159]

News of Fitzhugh's success traveled far and wide, and he was able to gather several more boats and crewmen for his commerce raiding. One of his next plans was to destroy the Wolf Trap Lightship in the Chesapeake Bay and seize any unsuspecting vessels that wandered his way. Upon hearing this threat, Lieutenant Peter Hayes of the North Atlantic Blockading Squadron sent a warning to the Wolf Trap Lightship and the York River oyster fleet. Hayes also ordered a boat to man the mouth of the Severn in Mobjack Bay, where he expected Fitzhugh to emerge. Rumors of Fitzhugh's objectives persisted; some said that he had four hundred men and fifteen large boats at his disposal. Informants believed that Fitzhugh was in Northern Neck with canoes, ready to attack the Chesapeake from Indian Creek and Dymer Creek.[160] There were also rumors that Rice Airs, a well-known plunderer, had set out with 154 guerrillas in several boats from Little Wicomico River for Smith Island. Airs's exploits were said to have included his participation in John Taylor Wood's raid on the *Reliance* in 1863. Acting ensign Thomas Nelson described Airs and his men as "a most desperate set of thieves, robbers and murderers, who [used] the cloth of the rebel flag to cover their crimes....Their design on the island [was] to rob the stores...and probably capture some steamer, with which they [intended] to attack and destroy the light vessel and even surprise the blockading vessels."[161] The rumors about Airs forced Secretary Gideon Welles to extend the Potomac Flotilla's jurisdiction and to increase its size to thirty-one ships.

Although the rumors about Airs never materialized, the ones about Fitzhugh came true. In April 1865, Fitzhugh led a raiding party that committed what was supposedly the last piratical act in the Chesapeake Bay during the Civil War. General Robert E. Lee asked Fitzhugh whether a Union transport vessel laden with supplies for General Grant's army could be seized and run into a certain inlet for the Confederate army. Fitzhugh informed Lee that it was, indeed, possible and that he would undertake the mission. Fitzhugh was given a detail of forty men and the offer of "whatever assistance" he needed from the Confederate navy. He was directed to go into the Chesapeake Bay, near the mouth of the Rappahannock, in whatever boats he could procure; from there, he was to proceed up the bay to a point that would promise the capture of the steamers the *Highland Light* and the *Harriet De Ford*. A copy of the *Baltimore Gazette* noted that a point below Annapolis was where Fitzhugh last stopped.[162]

After receiving his mission, Fitzhugh procured three open boats and started sailing up the bay from Wind-Mill Point on the north side of the Rappahannock. He reached the Potomac River the next morning and remained there for two days. On the third night, the wind and tide became favorable, so Fitzhugh moved on and kept his vessels close to the shore. Around sunrise the next morning, the men reached Cedar Point near the

The Pending Conflict, a political cartoon critical of the European abetment of the Confederate war effort and of the anti-Lincoln and pacifist movement in the North, circa 1864. *Courtesy of the Library of Congress Prints and Photographs Division.*

mouth of the Patuxent River, where they hid their boats and rested. While his men rested, Fitzhugh and one of his men went into a small village and reported that they were deserters from Grant's army who wanted to go to Baltimore in order to learn the whereabouts of the two Union steamers. The men learned from the locals that the *Harriet De Ford* was heading down the river to Baltimore the next day; on its journey, the ship was planning to stop at the town of Marlborough. Fitzhugh knew that a telegraph line ran from

Marlborough to Point Lookout and Washington, D.C., so he decided that it wouldn't be safe for his men to capture the ship in Marlborough. Instead, he planned to wait until the *Harriet De Ford* landed in Fair Haven, which is around fourteen miles south of Annapolis.[163]

As night fell, Fitzhugh and his men launched their boats—the wind and tide were again in their favor—and they moved up the bay as fast as they could. Fitzhugh and his men reached Herring Bay the following morning around 4:00 a.m., and he found that it was dotted with lights from the mastheads of numerous anchored vessels. He chose the largest and most isolated of these vessels for seizure before the *Harriet De Ford* arrived. His men imprisoned the ship's crew below deck while they "feasted on fine oysters with which [the ship] was about one-third loaded." Fitzhugh then equipped nineteen of his best men with the clothes of the boat's crewmembers for a reconnaissance mission on shore. During this mission, they learned that the *Highland Light*, one of the fastest ships in the bay, was supposed to be landing at a wharf on West River, which was just a few miles away from Fair Haven. After hearing this information, Fitzhugh secured a wagon for the men and told them to make their way down the Eastern Shore; all the while, they were also supposed to pretend to be woodchoppers looking for work. Unfortunately for Fitzhugh, the men arrived at the wharf just as the steamer was moving downriver and out into the bay, so they returned to Fair Haven to await the arrival of the *Harriet De Ford*.[164]

They didn't have to wait long. As soon as the ship landed, Fitzhugh's men went on board again and passed themselves off as woodchoppers who were seeking passage to Baltimore. Once they were on board, Fitzhugh placed his men in command positions all around the boat, "from the engine room to the pilothouse." When they were about five miles from shore, Fitzhugh went into the pilothouse, exposed his Confederate uniform and arms and demanded the surrender of the boat "in the name of the Confederate States." The captain of the *Harriet De Ford* saw that resistance was futile and quickly ordered the surrender of the ship. Back at the wharf, Fitzhugh sent out all the noncombatants from the boat's crew and demanded "their parole of honor to give [them] such time as to get down the bay in safety." As Fitzhugh and his men made their way through the bay, they heard heavy gunfire from both Annapolis and Washington, D.C. This was meant to honor the capture of Petersburg and the fall of Richmond. Knowing that General Lee had changed the location of his base—"rendering the object of the expedition futile"— Fitzhugh hurried his men down the bay "as fast as steam" could take

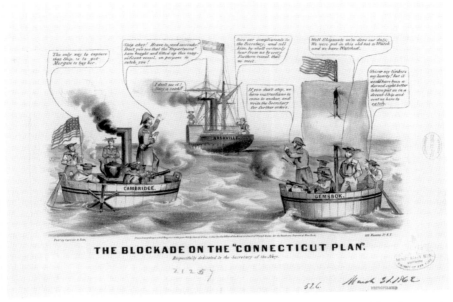

The blockade on the "Connecticut Plan," a political cartoon by Currier and Ives that mocks the government's early efforts to overhaul and augment a somewhat outdated Union fleet to blockade Southern ports and effectively defend against Confederate privateers and blockade runners, circa 1862. *Courtesy of the Library of Congress Prints and Photographs Division.*

them in order to get back to Lee's army. Fitzhugh and his men had captured two vessels, one steamer, one cannon, sixty-two stands of small arms, valuable stores and 205 prisoners, including 60 black men, and he did all of this without suffering a single loss.[165]

When the district commander of Annapolis learned of Fitzhugh's success, he telegraphed the officers at Fort Monroe, Point Lookout and Baltimore. He sent ten Potomac Flotilla vessels in pursuit of him with the order to "be prepared to sink the *De Ford* should you fall in with her." As Fitzhugh and his men were unloading their cargo, seven U.S. gunboats came upon them and began shelling the shore. Fitzhugh and his men hurriedly unloaded as much as they could before they set fire to the *Harriet De Ford* and escaped into the woods. Whatever plans Fitzhugh and his men had to capture other steamers and "to burn and pillage generally" were dashed with the end of the war.[166]

END OF THE WAR

On April 9, 1865, General Robert E. Lee surrendered the Army of Northern Virginia to General Ulysses S. Grant at Appomattox Courthouse. After Lee was forced to abandon Richmond, the capital of the Confederacy, he found himself harassed by U.S. cavalrymen and unable to join other Confederate troops in North Carolina. Lee felt that he had no other option than to surrender; otherwise, he would have suffered a humiliating and deadly defeat. With the end of the war came the end of commerce raiding at the hands of Confederate privateers and naval officials, and the Chesapeake was once again at peace.

PART V

THE PEARL OF THE CHESAPEAKE: THE OYSTER WARS

1865-1959

*M*arch 2018 marked 150 years since the establishment of Maryland's "Oyster Navy," a forerunner of today's Maryland Department of Natural Resources Police.[167] The group was necessary for dealing with the lucrative, competitive and sometimes deadly industries that operated in the Chesapeake Bay. By the mid-nineteenth century, the waterfront societies of the Chesapeake Bay had reached maturity, and their economies were intimately tied to their successes on the water. Residents of the Chesapeake Bay area were so dependent on the bay that one visitor from Philadelphia remarked, "[They could] almost be called an amphibious race; for nearly all the men and boys spend their lives on the water."[168]

Oysters, in particular, were the residents' main draw to the water, which earned them the nickname "oyster catchers" from the merchants in Baltimore. Oyster fishing was good business; it was so successful that fishermen from as far away as New England flocked to the bay, which led to an over-abundance of competition. The Maryland waters of the Chesapeake Bay are particularly ideal for growing oysters due to their vast expanses, suitable temperatures and salinity levels. The Maryland area's waters also had few oyster predators and were free of the parasites that cause common oyster diseases. Maryland wanted to stop the influx of outside competition, so in 1830, it passed a series of laws that limited Maryland oyster harvesting to in-state residents only. There were also laws passed concerning the two types of oyster catching: tonging and dredging. Those who used the tonging

Two men on a police boat arresting two men who are illegally oystering on Chesapeake Bay, off Swan's Point. In *Frank Leslie's Illustrated Newspaper* from a sketch by Frank Adams, circa 1888. *Courtesy of the Library of Congress Prints and Photographs Division.*

method worked in shallower waters, and their boats generally carried only a couple of men; one of the men would use long tongs to gather the oysters and one would cull them. Maryland officials outlawed dredging, a harvesting method that was considered harmful to the bay, although Virginia continued to permit it until 1879. Dredgers used larger boats and worked in deeper waters, where they would harvest oysters in basketlike scoops that they dragged over the oyster beds. Dredging often left so few oysters that they could not naturally reproduce fast enough. So, when out-of-state watermen brought their dredges to the Chesapeake, Maryland lawmakers were concerned.[169] Some say that the passage of these laws was the start of the so-called Oyster Wars. In Maryland and Virginia, anyone who violated the oyster laws became known in the press as "oyster pirates."

When the Civil War erupted in 1861, Maryland and its oyster catchers remained members of the United States despite a large number of Southern sympathizers among their population. But just because they were loyal to the United States didn't mean they were going to put their profitable businesses on hold. They enjoyed a thriving illicit commercial relationship with the Confederate States. Some schooners were even employed by Richmond specifically as blockade runners. Despite the United States' attempt to stop the smuggling by placing gunboats throughout the bay, they were no match for the Chesapeake oyster catchers. By 1865, more legislation had passed. One law required harvesters to purchase an annual license because the General Assembly didn't want dredging or over-harvesting to destroy the oyster population. But enforcement of the laws was left to local authorities. And they had little ability to patrol the open water. That changed, however, in 1868 when Maryland created its State Oyster Police force, which was given the authority to enforce the laws.[170] After the Civil War, the oyster harvesting industry exploded. By the 1880s, the Chesapeake Bay supplied almost half of the world's supply of oysters. New England fishermen further encroached on the bay after their local oyster beds had been exhausted. This prompted violent clashes with competitors from Maryland and Virginia.

PRIME PICKIN'S

Although New Englanders were technically barred from catching oysters in the Chesapeake Bay, they were not stopped from setting up businesses in Baltimore. Men like Caleb Maltby found ways to enter the oyster industry through lucrative side-hustles. For example, Maltby owned the Maltby House Hotel in Baltimore Harbor; the hotel was a four-story building that served as the center of the Chesapeake Bay oyster industry. As a leading oyster broker, Maltby's hotel was a place where contracts were won and oyster prices were set. The establishment of such locations and oyster-packing houses also coincided with the building of the Baltimore and Ohio (B&O) Railroad, which allowed oyster packers to send shipments westward. On the eve of the Civil War, the B&O routinely carried over three million pounds of oysters to the West. Oysters proved to be a million-dollar industry, with nearly sixty packinghouses lining Baltimore's wharf.[171]

Despite a brief disruption in the Chesapeake Bay's legitimate economy during the Civil War, two developments at the war's end led to an unprecedented expansion of the industry. The first was the development of a steam-canning process, which allowed for the long-distance transport of oysters. The second was a booming postwar economy that enabled more people to purchase luxury and status-conferring commodities, including oysters. Even the Eastern Shore of Maryland felt the benefits of the oyster boom. Men like John Crisfield promoted the development of the Eastern Shore Railroad and acquired the rights to harvest oysters in Somers Cove. Crisfield believed that the Eastern Shore was on the threshold of the seafood boom, particularly Somers Cove, which is located at the gateway to Tangier Sound, one of the richest oyster grounds in the world. Between the railroad, land speculation and the oyster boom, Crisfield and his partners were bound to be filthy rich.

During the 1869 and 1870 oyster season, Maryland had 563 licensed oyster catchers who each caught, on average, twenty-three tons of oysters, each in eight-hundred-bushel loads. By 1870, oysters were selling for forty-five cents per bushel, and they were the anchor of a $50 million seafood industry. The captain of a dredger could earn $2,000 a year, while most Marylanders earned $500 or less each year. This economic boom resonated in Baltimore, where hundreds of "schooners, pungies and bateaux annually disgorged four million bushels of oysters." And by 1872, the town of Crisfield had the largest oyster trade in the state, which supplied employment for over 600 ships. Crisfield oysters were shipped to every corner of the United States and even traveled as far away as Europe and Australia. By 1880, almost 5,800 Virginia-based vessels were involved in the oyster trade.[172]

Of course, all of this prosperity bred competition, and sometimes, that competition turned violent. Fights and brawls were common occurrences in waterfront towns like Crisfield and Baltimore. Towns like Crisfield became known for their "honky-tonk, brawling den of swaggering watermen, prostitutes, drunkenness, violence and quick profits from oystering." Many of these early 1870s conflicts erupted between Virginians and Marylanders over border disputes and discontented tongers and dredgers. Virginia oyster harvesters would often travel into Maryland waters with blackened sails under the cover of darkness in order to illegally dredge in Maryland waters. Sometimes, Maryland's own men would poach in the rivers of neighboring counties. While Maryland counties had gradually loosened their laws regarding dredging—including their allowance of dredging in deep waters—by the 1870s, dredgers were notorious for defying the laws, and they often poached oysters in shallow waters. Watermen could usually distinguish one boat from another and could tell the boat's port county by things such as the cut of the sail or the rake of the mast.[173]

THE FIRST OYSTER WAR (1882–1883)

While there were plenty of fights and skirmishes between oyster catchers prior to 1882, the first "official" Oyster War was actually waged by Virginia governor William E. Cameron. This Oyster War was part of an ongoing conflict between the government of Virginia and the "lawless" oyster dredgers of the Chesapeake Bay, and the events that took place during this war were squarely within Virginia's borders. Much like the oyster boom in Maryland, the boom in Virginia's oyster industry after the Civil War forced the state's government to increase its emphasis on protective legislation. As early as 1878, scientific studies that were conducted by a U.S. Naval officer named Francis Winslow concluded that the oysters in the Chesapeake Bay were in danger of being overharvested. While on board a Maryland Oyster Navy vessel called the *Leila*, Winslow determined that the oysters were being taken from the bay at a rate far greater than could naturally replenish.

All of a sudden, Virginia's officials were concerned about overuse and the devastation that was wrought by dredging; they, like Maryland officials, were also concerned about non-Virginia oyster catchers depleting the state's valuable supply. Governor Cameron routinely received information about non-Virginia dredgers operating just a few miles north of Hampton Roads near the Rappahannock River. Violence also began rising between the wealthier oyster-dredgers and the "more numerous but less affluent" tongers, which resulted in several deaths. In 1880, dredging was outlawed in Virginia waters in an attempt to end these conflicts, but the well-armed and well-organized dredgers—many of whom were from Maryland—simply ignored the ban. Governor Cameron eventually grew tired of these perceived depredations and made his move.[174]

In February 1882, Cameron gathered a crew of volunteers and equipped them with "three days rations, an abundance of ammunition and three three-inch rifled guns." The governor, along with a staff of officers, even accompanied the volunteer troops aboard their ship, the *Victoria J. Peed*. In the meantime, local authorities installed a battery of long-range guns at the mouth of the Rappahannock River, and Cameron sent a company of the Richmond artillerymen to the scene. The goal of the battery was simple: force the oyster dredgers to surrender peacefully when they were confronted with such a display of force. Cameron believed that taking physical action would be more effective than trying to enforce the laws through empty threats and failed legal proceedings. When the *Victoria J. Peed* arrived at the mouth of the Rappahannock on February 17, 1882, its crew caught sight of a fleet of six oyster schooners and a single sloop, but Cameron couldn't yet take action, so he awaited the arrival of his other steamer, the *Louisa*, which was held up by foul weather.[175]

When the *Louisa* joined the *Victoria J. Peed* a few hours later, both of the vessels approached the oyster fleet. When the groups were just two miles apart, both the *Louisa* and the *Victoria J. Peed* moved into offensive positions in order to prevent the schooners from escaping justice. However, the governor also wanted to approach the suspected pirates without raising alarm, so he suggested a ruse: the two ships would pretend to be a tug and a disabled freighter; the *Victoria J. Peed* would be ready to attack, while the *Louisa* would be in a position to block escape attempts. According to a report in the *Norfolk Virginian* from February 19, 1882, when both of the ships were within a mile of the first oyster boat, General V.D. Groner aboard the *Victoria J. Peed* "ordered the men to fire a volley of musketry and one solid shot across the bow of the nearest schooner." Their plan was met with success. The first ship immediately surrendered to the crew of the *Victoria J. Peed*, and two of the others, the *Annie and Alice* and the *J.C.*, quickly followed suit. The *Louisa* was successful, too; it captured three schooners called the *Fashion*, the *E.D. Chandler* and the *Mary Tauline* and a sloop called *Hamburg*. Only one vessel, a schooner called the *Philip Kirkwood*, managed to flee from the melee. This escape set into motion a three-hour, thirty-five-mile pursuit of the *Philip Kirkwood* by the *Victoria J. Peed*. Despite the *Philip Kirkwood*'s head start, Governor Cameron and the men of the *Victoria J. Peed* easily overtook the *Philip Kirkwood*. Cameron's first raid was a resounding success.[176]

Fifty-nine dredgers were captured in the raid, and forty-six of them were sentenced to one year in prison. There were thirteen dredgers under the age of sixteen who were not prosecuted. The dredgers also had to forfeit their boats and repurchase them at auction, which netted the government a profit of $8,600. But none of the men served their full prison term; many of them "talked with tears in their eyes of wives and children, of mothers and sisters at home, and seemed to feel keenly the disgrace of their situation." So, Governor Cameron exercised his power of executive clemency and commuted the sentences of six of the dredge boat captains to just sixty days, and he freed the seventh, who was in ill health. He also issued pardons to the rest of the dredgers, with the exception of one: William Larken, who had set fire to the jail in his attempt to escape. Cameron's motivation for this show of mercy was as much about popularity—all but one of the ships hailed from Virginia's Eastern Shore—as it was about politics. Most of the men he seized were from Onancock in Accomack County, where Cameron had drawn a lot of support during his election. Cameron also, however, issued a firm statement of his intention to enforce the dredging laws and used this first raid as an example of what could happen to future offenders.[177]

Despite his successes, Cameron's popularity was short-lived. The governor received devastating news in November 1882, when the state supreme court of appeals decided that the boat owners from his February raid were entitled to a full refund of the money they had spent repurchasing their boats. According to the court, the owners were not adequately represented in the trial when compared to the representation of the captains and crews. It also turned out that the governor's show of force wasn't as effective in deterring future oyster pirates as he had hoped. In November 1882, he learned that a fleet of more than fifty oyster catchers had resumed dredging in Virginia waters and that a well-armed Maryland contingent and many of the watermen the governor had previously pardoned were among them.[178]

THE SECOND OYSTER WAR (1883–1884)

As a reaction to the growth of another dredging fleet, a second Oyster War began in February 1883. Governor Cameron prepared for a second raid in much the same way that he did for his first; he set his base of operations in Norfolk and used the city's militia units as his crew. He also called in the *Victoria J. Peed* again, but the flagship of his new fleet would be a steamer called the *Pamlico*. Once the preparations were done, Cameron, his staff, three newspaper reporters (one from the *New York Herald*, one from the *Norfolk Evening Ledger* and a stowaway from the *Norfolk Virginian*), thirty-five militiamen, the sheriff of Mathews County and numerous others joined the crew of the *Pamlico* on its maiden Oyster War voyage.

On February 27, the *Pamlico* and the rest of the governor's fleet set out late at night—just as the governor's crew had during the first Oyster War—to use the dark to their advantage. However, they immediately ran into problems. First, the *Pamlico* and the *Victoria J. Peed* became separated when the *Victoria J. Peed* stopped at the wreckage of the *Treadwell* just a few miles up the bay. This was likely done as a ruse similar to the one that Governor Cameron had successfully used before. Second, unexpectedly rough seas overturned a stove in the *Pamlico*'s main cabin, which spewed smoke and hot coals all over the sleeping militiamen. Two of the men, Captain Gilmer and Lieutenant Lee, were injured trying to throw the stove overboard. Third, the rough seas also caused many of the men to suffer from severe seasickness; one of them even said that the oyster pirates "could have the [damned] oysters if they want 'em." Fourth—and most importantly—the men learned the following morning that advance warning had been given to the dredgers. With the arrival of that warning, most of the oyster pirates sailed into Maryland waters before the raiders even had the chance to arrive. Since there were three members of the press aboard the ships, all of the raid's embarrassing moments were printed and shared widely.[179]

Governor Cameron thought his luck had turned, however, when a reconnaissance mission along the coast of Northumberland County discovered that there were eight schooners near the mouth of the Potomac River. The captain of the *Pamlico* directed his crew to bear down on the fleet of oyster pirates, who immediately began to scatter. Before they could even reach them, the *Victoria J. Peed* temporarily ran aground, giving all but one of the oyster pirates the opportunity to flee to Maryland waters. The unfortunate oyster harvesters who were aboard the *Palo Alto* from Criswell accidentally ran their own vessel aground while they were trying to outrun the *Pamlico*. During the chase, the governor directed a barrage of twenty-four cannonballs and three hundred musket shots at the ship, but none of them hit the *Palo Alto*. The captain and first mate of the *Palo Alto* fled to Maryland in a rowboat, leaving behind a crew of six black men and one white man. Cameron secured the *Palo Alto* as a lawful prize.[180]

Still reeling from the loss of over fifty oyster pirate ships, Governor Cameron was determined that his next raid would not be a wasted effort. When the men of the *Pamlico* witnessed the crew of another potential pirate vessel, the *Dancing Molly*, searching for wood on the shore, the governor hoped that their attack would be easily executed. What Cameron didn't know was that the captain had brought his wife and two daughters along with him and that they had remained inside the dredge boat when the men went ashore. All three of the women were skilled seafarers themselves, so when the *Pamlico* began to approach the *Dancing Molly*, the women ignored the warning shots, took advantage of the winds in their favor and escaped to Maryland. According to the *Norfolk Virginian*, spectators along the Virginia shore "really wished for the safety of the tiny craft" after they realized it was crewed by three women, "and when the *Dancing Molly* got safely out, the group of Virginians chivalrously gave three cheers for the pirate's wife and daughters." This was a particularly humiliating defeat for the governor.[181]

Despite his losses, the governor was not ready to give up just yet. He ordered the *Pamlico* to return to Norfolk with the *Palo Alto*, and he shifted his efforts to the *Victoria J. Peed*. This proved to be a much more successful venture; on March 1, 1883, Cameron intercepted five schooners off Pungoteague Creek on the Eastern Shore. None of the captains attempted to flee, as they were all Virginians and argued that they had not broken Virginia law. Instead, the captains claimed that they were crossing the bay into the Maryland portion of the Potomac River, where dredging was legal. But Governor Cameron refused to believe the men and turned them over as pirates to the authorities in Accomack and Mathews Counties. Of course, insufficient evidence resulted in their immediate acquittals—yet another humiliation for the governor. His embarrassment continued to grow in April 1883, when the Northumberland County grand jury refused to indict the crewmen of the *Palo Alto*.[182]

Although Governor Cameron did not lead any additional raids in the Chesapeake, he did attempt to deal with the continued outbursts of violence among the oyster harvesters through legislation. In February 1884, he informed lawmakers that the state's losses from oyster piracy totaled a minimum of $2 million per year. After realizing that real damage was being done to the state's economy, Virginia lawmakers enacted a bill that established the Board on the Chesapeake and Its Tributaries. This administrative agency was authorized to "purchase, arm and staff a permanent naval police force to protect the commonwealth's oyster interests." The board's members included the governor, the auditor of public accounts and the state treasurer, and it was initially financed with $30,000. There is no doubt that this organization took some notes from Maryland's Oyster Navy, and it worked. In just one year, the Virginia oyster police seized sixty-one boats for violations, and the state tax revenues from the watermen increased from practically nothing to more than $26,000 during the 1884 and 1885 fiscal year. Although the enforcement problems were not entirely eliminated, improvements were made.[183]

H.P. CANNON AND THE *MAUD MULLER*

In February 1884, the *New York Times* received a dispatch from Baltimore about "interesting developments" in the Oyster Wars of the Chesapeake Bay. From the deck of a Maryland Oyster Police boat called the *Leila*, a *New York Times* reporter recounted a situation that he felt indicated "that serious trouble and probably bloodshed [would] ensue before the existing difficulties [were] ended, if, indeed, the authorities [would] be able to cope with the pirates at all." The pirates' depredations, he said, had grown "bolder and bolder," and he said that the Oyster Police had revealed themselves to be ineffective at suppressing the actions of the oyster pirates. The incident that was recounted by this reporter happened when the oyster fleet reached Goose Creek and turned a captured dredger called the *Maud Muller* over to Justice Robinson. The owner of the boat, Sylvester Cannon, managed to escape, but his father, H.P. Cannon—the "Pirate Chief"—did not. When H.P. learned that there was no warrant charging him with a specific offense, he went "boldly ashore, and with characteristic piratical boldness, walked on board the steamer *Leila.*" He had four loaded revolvers with him.[184]

Unfortunately for the Oyster Police, H.P. had been a civil magistrate at one time, so he was familiar with the law. He demanded the immediate release of the *Maud Muller* on account that the seizure of the boat was illegal, since the owner had not been captured on it. Justice Robinson's hands were tied, so the ship was released. Unaware of his father's legal maneuverings, Sylvester Cannon fired shots in the direction of the police boat as his father was sailing the *Maud Muller* out of the harbor. The captain of *Leila* immediately ordered a raid on the shore to find Sylvester Cannon, but Cannon eluded him as he made his way to Justice Robinson's house. With weapons drawn, Cannon "intimidated" the household's members as he thoroughly searched the premises and swore to kill Justice Robinson on sight. Upon finding that Robinson was not home, Cannon left—but not without promising to return. The ladies of the home sought assistance from their neighbors, because they feared that Cannon would make good on his threat. So, when Cannon returned, he found "several armed men in the house" and "withdrew in company with several of his brothers, who had joined him." While they were hiding in the thick forest, Cannon and his brothers barraged the Robinsons' home—as well as the police boat—with bullets. So many shots were fired that the captain of the police boat thought that there must have been a riot on shore and sent ten armed men to the wharf to suppress it.[185]

As the police force tried to land, the pirates observed their approach and continued spraying bullets at them until they escaped into the swamp. Although the police conducted a thorough search for Cannon and his brothers, it was eventually abandoned when they were nowhere to be found. The *New York Times* correspondent described the Cannon brothers as "desperate characters" and claimed that Sylvester Cannon narrowly escaped death when he was shot while illegally dredging for oysters. His brother Alexander had stripped one of his own crewmen and placed him on the deck in midwinter, and his frozen corpse was later found. His other brothers, Milburn and Charley, had also been involved in multiple shooting cases. The correspondent most fortuitously had the opportunity to interview H.P. Cannon about his piratical acts and those of his sons. He said:

> *If I am a pirate, I was driven to it by the authorities, who permitted men to work these beds with rebuke. Within the last two weeks, I have seen $100,000 worth of damage done to the oyster beds of Fishing Bay, which may have been prevented if it had not been for the cowardice of Captain Insley and his crew. The illegal dredgers first descended upon Deal's Island. I wanted them arrested and volunteered to assist Captain Insley in a night attack. He consented, but when the dredgers began firing, he hove to and left me and my own to brave the brunt of the fight. The firing was so heavy that our sails were riddled and my crew compelled to go down below to escape the bullets. Our men, seeing there was no protection, then dredged wherever we found the best oysters.*[186]

The correspondent noted that a "bitter feud" existed between "the law and order party" and the "outlaws," who were "some two hundred in number." At that time, he argued that recent events promised "to develop into a startling climax." The state's leaders were heavily armed and openly threatened to shoot the pirates on sight, while the sheriff summoned a special posse to serve writs on the Cannon family. A rumor also persisted that Captain Insley had arranged a duel with Sylvester Cannon, who declined. The *Leila*, the correspondent said, would continue its war against the pirates.[187]

THE DEADLIEST OYSTER WAR (1888–1894)

In 1884, Maryland watermen hauled fifteen million bushels of oysters out of the Chesapeake Bay. By 1889, that number had gone down to fewer than ten million. In a study conducted by Dr. William K. Brooks, the director of the Chesapeake Zoological Laboratory and a professor of biology at Johns Hopkins University, he remarked that the Chesapeake would go bankrupt if the oysters were to give out. Between the improvements made in boating

The Oyster War in the Chesapeake depicted in *The Pirates Attacking the Police Schooner "Julia Hamilton"* by Schell and Hogan in *Harper's Weekly*, circa 1884. *Courtesy of the Library of Congress Prints and Photographs Division.*

and oyster processing technology and the overall increased demand for oysters, the number of oyster harvesters around the bay was becoming much too high. In Maryland, for example, profits from oysters were becoming so thin that the oyster harvesters were having difficulty paying for their expensive boats and equipment, so they turned to harvesting young oysters that were less than three inches long to fill their profit gap. The widespread use of oyster shells in limekilns and fertilizer plants also meant that reseeding, or placing seed oysters into the bed to regenerate, the beds was becoming impossible.[188]

Despite their earlier rivalry, the governments of Maryland and Virginia began to realize the need for cooperation in stamping out oyster piracy. In the late 1880s, the Maryland Oyster Navy was placed under new leadership; James F. Maddell kept a flotilla of three steamers and ten schooners in the Bay for 150 days a year. Despite the problems that continued to haunt the Maryland Oyster Navy, it became a true force to be reckoned with by 1900.[189]

WILLIAM FRANK WHITEHOUSE AND THE *ALBERT NICKEL*

At around 1:00 a.m. on the morning of February 19, a police sloop commanded by Captain George W. Clarke of the Oyster Navy arrived in the port of Annapolis; the vessel was called the *Folly*. Clarke had a prize with him: the pirate oyster schooner from Baltimore called the *Albert Nickel*. On the deck of the *Albert Nickel* was the body of its captain, William Frank Whitehouse; he had a single bullet wound on his left temple and a sixteen-shooter at his side. According to eyewitness reports, "the blood from the dead Captain's wound made a crimson stream along the bulwarks of the vessel." The sixteen repeating rifles and countless number of empty shells scattered nearby lent a warlike appearance to the scene. The event "made a tremendous sensation" in Annapolis, and it was the "first real tragedy in the history of the Oyster Navy."[190]

Captain Clarke and the *Folly* were assigned to the oyster grounds of Anne Arundel County, which were the ones closest to Baltimore. Throughout the year, Clarke had "considerable trouble" with the oyster pirates and several "lively skirmishes," but no one had been killed until the unfortunate incident that involved William Frank Whitehouse. In fact, "in all the previous history of the Oyster Navy, it has never killed anyone."

While Whitehouse's death may have been the first, it certainly was not the last. The purpose of the battles was more to intimidate rather than injure, but they still required a "great deal of gunpowder." It was only a matter of time before someone was killed.

The Whitehouse incident started at about 8:00 p.m. on February 18; the *Folly* was lying off Hackett's Point, just north of the mouth of the Severn River. About a mile from Sandy Point "came the sound of the falling and winding of dredgers," which could only have meant one thing: illegal dredging was happening at the oyster bar. So, Captain Clarke weighed anchor and set sail.[191] As Clarke approached the area of Sandy Point, he saw seven vessels. One man asked Clarke what he was going to do when someone from aboard the *Albert Nickel* ordered everyone to stand their ground, surround Clarke "and don't let him take [them]."

When Clarke approached the *Albert Nickel*, he ordered the ship to heave to, but the captain refused and instead "put on more sail to make off." In the meantime, the other pirate vessels maneuvered to place the *Folly* in the middle of them, but Captain Clarke was able to avoid the ambush by tacking out, and he kept up with the *Albert Nickel*. When he was within thirty yards of the *Albert Nickel*, Captain Clarke again demanded Captain Whitehouse to heave to, but he did not. So, Clarke, "as is customary in such cases, ordered his men to fire into the rigging" of the *Albert Nickel*. At that point, Whitehouse and his crew, joined by two other dredgers, opened fire on the *Folly*. For "ten minutes, the *Folly* engaged three vessels in a hand-to-hand fight of the warmest character." Bullets were flying wildly about, striking the sails of the *Folly*, whistling past the heads of the crew and cutting the rigging, but the pirates held their own in this most disadvantageous position.[192]

As the *Albert Nickel* drew close, Captain Clarke jumped aboard the ship with a revolver in his hand. The ship's crew of ten immediately surrendered to him, and Clarke placed them in the hold of the ship. At that point, Clarke was informed that Captain Whitehouse had died. The captain was lying on the deck of his ship with a bullet hole in his left temple and empty shells all around him; two cartridges were still in his rifle. During an examination of Whitehouse's wound, it was concluded that the bullet had entered his left temple and passed through the back of his head near the base of his brain; Whitehouse's death was most likely instantaneous.

Whitehouse's crew was placed in jail after confessing to a plot to use four dredging vessels to drive Clarke off the grounds. Whitehouse had been born in Norfolk, Virginia, but lived in Baltimore. He left behind a widow and five children, but he was still found guilty of dredging at night on forbidden grounds. The case raised important legal questions, which government officials expected to be "stoutly contested." One of those questions included who should be held responsible for Whitehouse's crime. Since the case was the first of its kind, and "the fact that the dead captain's friends [were] well to do," no one knew where to place the blame. It is unclear what ultimately happened to the unfortunate crew of the *Albert Nickel*.[193]

GUS RICE AND THE *J. C. MAHONEY*

One of the most formidable Chesapeake Bay oyster pirates was a man named Gus Rice, who lived "by his wits and his fists." During his career, Rice was hired as the captain of the *J.C. Mahoney*, a pungy boat owned by a Baltimore oyster speculator. Rice was a well-known leader of the oyster pirates, particularly those in the Chester River. According to descriptions, his "purple-red weathered face…and his rough growth of beard made him look every inch the killer he was." Rice once vowed that "no man would prevent him from catching oysters," and he even plotted to murder Hunter Davidson, the former leader of the Oyster Navy. Rice's crew was made up of men from the docks of Baltimore and the jails of the Eastern Shore. In the winter of 1887, despite new leadership and a renewed vigor, the Oyster Navy had significant difficulty dealing with Rice and his flotilla as they raided the oyster beds of the Chester River with impunity.[194]

Rice's plan was simple and straightforward: only work on moonlit nights and avoid being surprised. At the top of a pirate's mast was a globe light that would be lowered when a vessel from the Oyster Navy was sighted; this was meant as a signal to other boats. But there were two types of oyster pirates: those who worked until the Oyster Navy appeared and those who stood their ground and fought back. There was a fortune to be made with the oysters in the Chester River, so Rice's men were accustomed to fighting both the Oyster Navy and the tongers. The competition in the Chester River was so fierce that, in the spring of 1888, the tongers mounted a pair of cannons on the shore in an attempt to drive away the illicit dredge boats. Unfortunately, the men in charge of the cannons were "so inept that they were incapable of hitting anything with their one-pounders." Initially, Rice and the other pirates ignored the cannons, but on one April night, after a good haul and a lot of celebratory whiskey, Rice and the *J.C. Mahoney* decided to send a raiding party to shore to seize the cannons.[195]

As the men reached the fortress that contained the cannons, they learned that only a single watchman was in charge. Rice cruelly ordered the man to strip, and he sent the naked, terrified and humiliated man to Kent and Queen Anne's Counties with a message: "It [will] take more than two one-pounders and a sleeping watchman to keep Gus Rice out of the Chester River." Rice's men stole the cannons and placed them on the *J.C. Mahoney*. So much pressure was put on the state legislature after this incident that Annapolis dispatched the *Helen M. Baughman* to patrol the Chester River. All of Rice's fleet eluded the *Helen M. Baughman*, except for the *Kite*. While seizing the *Kite* was considered a success, the reality was that Rice was still operating throughout the river. But he was about to make a very costly mistake.[196]

One night, Rice and his men caught sight of a ship in the fog that looked like an Oyster Navy vessel. Rice ordered his men to fire upon it, and their bullets "whined and crashed through the steamer's cabins." But it turned out that the ship wasn't an Oyster Navy vessel at all; it was a passenger boat called the *Corsica* that was owned by the Baltimore and Eastern Shore Line. The *Corsica* was filled with women and children "who had feared for their lives as the storm of bullets hit the vessel." This incident was the last straw and sparked widespread anger. Baltimore and Annapolis newspapers demanded justice and an end to Rice's piratical depredations. The Oyster Navy soon received an order from the governor's office to send the *McLane*, its flagship steamer, to the Chester River. The *McLane* was captained by Thomas C.B. Howard, had a twelve-pound howitzer on its deck and was filled with men and rifles.[197]

Captain T.C.B Howard and the Oyster Pirates of the Chester River

In the late 1880s, the Chester River oyster beds were some of the "greatest natural treasures of the bay country." There, local watermen harvested thousands of bushels of oysters a year, and Kent County prospered. There were over one hundred tongers who worked in the mouth of the Chester River, but as the bay's oyster supply rapidly declined, pirate dredgers "invaded the Chester, and the crack of Winchesters resounded across the water." Captain T.C.B. Howard of the steamer *McLane* from the Maryland fishery force recounted one particularly difficult battle with the oyster pirates that took place in December 1888. Howard and his crew had left Annapolis on a Monday afternoon for the Chester River. Howard had heard about the repeated depredations in the area. When they arrived around 7:00 p.m., Howard found a fleet of about ten or fifteen boats at Wickes Beach. Although Howard was certain that they were pirate dredgers, he continued up the river, where he found an even larger fleet anchored at Hale's Point. There was one schooner that was headed downriver; Howard boarded it expecting to find unculled oysters, but there were none. So, Howard and his men continued on their way toward Judge Robinson's home, where they found three or four more boats dredging near one another.[198]

Howard called to one of the boats to haul down its jib, but the captain ignored Howard's order; Howard again called for him to haul down the jib, but he was again ignored. So, Howard and his crew opened fire, first in the rigging and then into the cabin. It was then that the captain of the pirate dredge called for quarter. The two boats that were closest to this pirate dredge hauled down their sails. One of the captains said that the "balls came too hot for him....He didn't want any aboard his boat." To the windward of this fleet—on Piney Point Bar—Captain Howard saw fifteen or twenty more dredgers at work, so he started upriver again, despite the fact that the dredgers had gained a considerable head start. The first vessel tacked westward and ran ashore while Howard's crew fired on it. Just beyond the first ship, Howard and his crew boarded a schooner and found unculled oysters. They arrested the crew, put a man on board to keep watch and started downriver, where the other members of the fleet were headed. Howard followed in hot pursuit; he met and anchored two more boats before starting back upriver. Howard was hell-bent on capturing as many pirate dredgers as he could."[199]

As the moon rose overhead, Howard saw ten or twelve boats coming down the river "in a solid body, showing red and green lights." This, according to Howard, meant that the pirate dredgers were prepared for a fight, so he told his men to get their rifles ready and properly loaded but not to shoot until given the order. In total, Howard had seven men on deck; they each "shot a great deal." When Howard approached boats, he ordered them all to haul down their jibs, but—as with the previous pirate fleet—these dredgers ignored the command. So, he ordered his men to fire across the bows of the pirate vessels, and the pirates responded and "promptly returned the fire." But, together, the dredgers were so well fortified that neither the rifles' fire nor the howitzers had any effect on them. So, Howard hauled across their bows, "barely avoiding collision," and put the cannon in a position to fire at the center of the fleet. Once it was lined up, Howard gave the order to fire. The cannon was loaded with grape and canister, and when it was fired, it struck at half-mast and did "great damage to spars, rigging and sails."[200]

The other dredgers "rattled away" at Howard and his crew, which made it difficult for them to reload the cannon. But they were able to successfully reload it, run under their sterns and, when they were just twenty feet from the pirates, fire again into the center of the fleet. This shot "raked and tore the sails." Another barrage of bullets was exchanged between the *McLane* and the pirate dredgers, so Howard ordered his men to reload the cannon and told them that he was going to "run into [the pirates]." The steamer had an iron bow, which could do considerable damage to the wooden dredge boats, so Howard literally ran into them, "striking the *Julia Jones* on the starboard quarter and letting the cannon go at the same time." As Howard backed out, one dredger jumped aboard the *McLane* and immediately surrendered to save his life. Howard's mate Charles W. Frazier, who had been helping him steer, was hit when a bullet entered the pilothouse. The wound, fortunately, proved to not be fatal.[201]

Howard pressed on; he ran to the windward of the dredgers, "hauled dead for them and struck the *J.C. Mahoney* on her port quarter." This time, however, he got hung up and could not back out, so he went ahead with full force and turned the *J.C. Mahoney* on its beam ends to clear it. The *J.C. Mahoney* immediately began sinking. What Howard couldn't have known was that the ship's crewmembers who had been impressed into service were locked in the forepeaks of both the *Julia Jones* and the *J.C. Mahoney*. Its crewmembers—eight in total—clambered aboard the *McLane* and begged Howard to save them; they said that they "had had enough of dredging." In the meantime, another vessel—the *Jones*—had also sunk, which left about eight dredgers "pouring broadsides" into Howard and his men, who tried to return their fire as quickly as possible. Since he had succeeded in disrupting several of the pirate dredgers, Howard made the decision to back off, at which point the dredgers dispersed. As they scattered, they came within range of a fleet at Hale's Point, but because it was so dark, Howard did not want to shoot and hit the "innocent persons on the boats anchored there." Several of the pirate captains escaped, including the nefarious Gus Rice.[202]

Howard then made his way to Centreville, where he placed his prisoners in jail. The next day, they were tried for possessing unculled oysters. That evening, Howard and his crew returned to the scene of their previous battle and "laid all Tuesday night in a fleet of dredgers off Hale's Point." However, he saw no dredging. Maryland governor Elihu Emory Jackson "heartily approved of the battle conducted by Captain Howard" and remarked that "as long as there is any necessity for such proceedings," he gave Howard full support in getting things done.

After Howard's daring attack on the pirate dredgers, the city of Annapolis received a telegram from Baltimore about an assassination plot against Captain George W. Clarke. He was the captain of the *Folly*, which was on guard at Hackett's Point Oyster Bar, just four miles from Annapolis. The *McLane*, which required repairs to its boiler and cannon, was unable to assist Captain Clarke. So, the governor requested that the Naval Academy allow the state to use several steam launches and Gatling guns. The secretary of the navy, William Collins Whitney, approved, and Commander Sampson of the Naval Academy brought two steam launches: one armed with a howitzer and the other with a Gatling gun. The governor placed Captain Howard in command of one of the steam launches, and they made for Hackett's Point at once.[203]

CONCLUSION OF THE OYSTER WARS

There were countless skirmishes between oyster pirates and the oyster police forces of Maryland and Virginia throughout the late nineteenth and mid-twentieth centuries. The worse problem for oyster harvesters, however, was their failure to heed the warning of Dr. Brooks. During the winter of 1892 and 1893, there was a scarcity of oysters, and nine hundred dredgers scrambled to catch what they could. At this point, the governments of Maryland and Virginia slowly started taking more concerted steps toward regulating the industry. In Maryland, for example, the state legislature passed a culling law that prohibited harvesters from keeping oysters that measured less than two and one-half inches from hinge to mouth. The state also hired a dozen conservation-minded oyster inspectors to enforce the oyster laws. In Virginia, things turned dire, as pests, disease and pollution in the Norfolk–Hampton Roads area caused a serious decline in the oyster population. This decline affected the entire region; competition on the water intensified, and conflicts between different interest groups increased. By the turn of the century, there were more oyster packinghouses closing on the Chesapeake than there were opening, and one of the oyster inspectors, W.E. Revelle, reported that "a mean spirit prevailed among the people of the region."[204]

The Oyster War in the Chesapeake depicted in *Pirates Dredging at Night* by Schell and Hogan in *Harper's Weekly*, circa 1884. *Courtesy of the Library of Congress Prints and Photographs Division.*

The situation grew even more desperate in 1905, when nearly two hundred dredge boats sailed around Cape Charles to Sinepuxent Bay and poached undersized oysters. The Oyster Navy rushed to the scene, but it was too late; the oyster catchers had already severely damaged the Sinepuxent beds. In 1906, Maryland conducted a $200,000 survey to assess the condition of the oyster beds of the Chesapeake. The survey was directed by Charles C. Yates and spanned from June 1906 to August 1912; Yates and his men "triangulated, charted, buoyed and sampled over one million acres of Chesapeake bottom." During the survey, Maryland attempted to conserve the oysters and regulate the harvesting industry by leasing oyster beds; the first attempts of this went as far back as the initial regulation efforts of the 1830s. Through this method, Maryland would grant citizens who were interested in growing oysters one-acre leases; later, the lease would be amended to five acres. These leases, of course, were detested by the oyster harvesters, who believed the waters were public and could be used however they saw fit. Maryland legislator

B. Howard Haman from Baltimore introduced the Haman Act for oyster leasing and cultivation. The bill was easily passed through the legislature and created the Board of Shellfish Commissioners, which was directed to lease barren bottoms of the Chesapeake to any Marylander who would plant, shell and seed oysters for twenty years. However, the oyster pirates looked for ways to circumvent the act—legally or not.[205]

Lean times continued throughout the first World War. During the 1917–18 winter, foul weather caused severe disruptions in the oyster industry. Ice that was fourteen inches thick formed on the Choptank River, forcing the oyster harvesters to chop holes through it. The ice off of Tilghman Island was so strong that trucks could be driven over it. With the passage of Prohibition, the Maryland Oyster Navy was given a new task: catch rumrunners who were smuggling liquor along the Chesapeake. Initially, as the Great Depression set in, the oyster harvesters were initially unaffected; however, the hurricane of 1933 affected them deeply, as heavy flooding throughout the Chesapeake destroyed farms, businesses and homes. The rivers in the region dumped millions of gallons of fresh water into the bay, which destroyed thousands of acres of oyster beds. The livelihoods of the oyster harvesters on Tangier Sound were lost forever, as the oyster-harvesting industry never recovered from the hurricane. This desperate situation again led oyster harvesters to piracy, but by 1937, the Maryland Oyster Navy was so well equipped with machine guns that it easily overtook illegal dredgers. After the outbreak of World War II, many oyster harvesters left their old profession behind to join the shipyards and armed services. The bay remained relatively empty of oyster harvesters until the 1950s and the "mini oyster boom."[206]

The Oyster Wars took a final and deadly turn in April 1959. Berkeley Muse was a well-respected community leader of Colonial Beach who speculated in real estate, farmed and sometimes tonged oysters. On the fateful night of April 7, 1959, Muse's friend Harvey King invited him to dredge for oysters later that night. King reportedly said, "I don't give a damn about the police." And indeed, he didn't. So, Muse joined King and another man for a dredging trip around midnight. Unfortunately for them, the chief inspector of the Tidewater Fisheries Commission, Howard Shenton, had organized a stakeout on the river after receiving reports of illegal dredging. Shenton sent a PT boat called the *McKeldin* upstream and another called the *Honga River* to the mouth of Monroe Bay. The darkness of the early morning was further clouded by a mist that was rising off the water of the Potomac. King, Muse and their other friend had harvested about seven bushels of oysters by 4:30 a.m., when the mist began to clear and the sun began to rise.

At that time, the men caught sight of the *Honga River* heading toward them and made a beeline toward Monroe Bay. When the dredgers were just four hundred feet from the beach at Reno Pier, Shenton ordered his men to open fire. The Oyster Navy officers fired a half dozen warning shots at the speeding vessel. The *Honga River* had stopped chasing the men after it burned out a bearing in its engine, but the men saw that the *McKeldin* was also coming quickly for them. King attempted to maneuver their boat away, which put them on a collision course with the *Honga River*. The officers on board the *Honga River* continued firing at the men as the pirate boat swerved. Then, Berkeley Muse reportedly shouted "Oh! I've been hit!" He then collapsed and died on the culling board of the boat. Muse had been shot directly in the chest, while King had taken a bullet to the leg.[207]

Muse's death hit the community of Colonial Beach hard. As news spread of Muse's death "in a blaze of gunfire," the citizens of Colonial Beach demanded justice. After all, Muse and King had been unarmed, and the barrage of bullets was beyond the scope of warning shots. By 1959, so few men were dredging oysters at Colonial Beach that the residents were outraged. One resident, Calvin Dickinson, said, "To deliberately shoot a man in 1959 for taking oysters was going too far." The Maryland Oyster Navy officers were warned to stay away from the Virginia shore. Due to their actions, the oyster harvesters believed that the Oyster Navy aimed to kill them, not just disable their engines. In response to the public outcry from this attack, the commissioner of the Potomac River Fisheries, H.C. Byrd, disbanded the Oyster Navy in 1959, as it was too controversial and clearly ineffective. And so it was that the tragic death of Berkeley Muse marked the end of the Chesapeake Bay Oyster Wars.[208]

GLOSSARY

appurtenance: An accessory or other item that is associated with a particular activity or style of living.

brigantine: A two-masted sailing vessel with a fully square-rigged foremast and at least two sails on the main mast: a square topsail and a gaff sail mainsail (behind the mast). The main mast is the second and taller of the two masts.

careen: To turn (a ship) on its side for cleaning, caulking or repair.

dragnet: A system of coordinated measures for apprehending criminals or other individuals.

drogher: A sailing barge used in the West Indian coastal trade or a clumsy cargo boat especially of coasting type.

forepeak: The extreme forward lower compartment or tank that is usually used for trimming or storage in a ship.

frigate: Any warship built for speed and maneuverability. The description that is often used is "frigate-built." These could be warships carrying their principal batteries of carriage-mounted guns on a single deck or on two decks (with smaller carriage-mounted guns on the forecastle and quarterdeck of the vessel).

fustic: A type of dyestuff.

galley: A type of ship that is propelled mainly by rowing. The galley is characterized by its long, slender hull, shallow draft and low freeboard (clearance between sea and railing).

grapeshot: A geometric arrangement of round shot packed tightly into a canvas bag and separated from the gunpowder charge by a metal disk of full-bore diameter. Grapeshot used fewer larger projectiles than were contained within canisters or shrapnel shells.

heave to: A way of slowing a sailboat's forward progress, as well as a way to fix the helm and sail positions so that the boat does not have to be steered.

hogshead: A large cask that is smaller than a barrel.

impressment: Being forced through some means of coercion.

jib: A triangular staysail set forward of the forwardmost mast.

lightship: A moored or anchored vessel with a beacon light to warn or guide ships at sea.

lignum vitae: A type of wood.

man-of-war: A British Royal Navy expression for a powerful warship or frigate from the era between the sixteenth and nineteenth centuries. Although the term never acquired a specific meaning, it was usually reserved for a ship armed with cannons and propelled primarily by sails, as opposed to a galley, which was primarily propelled by oars.

picaroon: A pirate or privateer from the archaic meaning of "rogue" or "scoundrel."

pink: Any small ship with a narrow stern, having derived from the Dutch word *pincke*, which means pinched. They had a large cargo capacity and were generally square rigged. Their flat bottoms (and resulting shallow draught) made them more useful in shallow waters than some similar classes of ship.

pinnace: A light boat—propelled by oars or sails—carried aboard merchant and war vessels in the Age of Sail to serve as a tender. The pinnace was usually rowed but could be rigged with a sail for use in favorable winds.

port: The side of the vessel that is to the left of an observer facing the bow—that is, facing in the direction that the vehicle is heading when underway.

PT boat: A patrol torpedo boat, or a torpedo-armed fast attack vessel.

pungy: A type of schooner unique to the Chesapeake Bay region. The name is believed to derive from the Pungoteague region of Accomack County, Virginia, where the design was developed in the 1840s and 1850s.

scow: A flat-bottomed boat used for transporting cargo to and from ships in harbor.

scuttle: To deliberately sink a ship by allowing water to flow into the hull.

shallop: Typically refers to a small, open boat propelled by oars or sails that is used primarily in shallow waters.

shallow-draft boat: A boat with a keel that is not far below the waterline.

sloop: A one-masted sailboat with a fore-and-aft mainsail and a jib.

snow: A square-rigged vessel with two masts, complemented by a snow- or trysail-mast stepped immediately abaft (behind) the main mast.

starboard: The side of the vessel that is to the right of an observer facing the bow.

tacking: A sailing maneuver by which a vessel, whose desired course is into the wind, turns its bow toward the wind so that the direction from which the wind blows changes from one side to the other, allowing progress in the desired direction.

tierce: Refers to a cask that is intermediate in size between the barrel and the hogshead.

tipple: An alcoholic drink.

NOTES

Introduction

1. Robert Brenner, *Merchants and Revolution: Commercial Change, Political Conflict, and London's Overseas Traders* (London: Verso, 2003), 120–21.

2. "America and West Indies," *Calendar of State Papers Colonial, America and West Indies Vol. 10, 1677–1680* (March 1677): 1–15, commission signed by Sir George Yeardley, governor and captain-general of Virginia, to "my well-beloved friend William Claiborne."

3. Ibid., commission signed by John Pott, governor and captain-general of Virginia, to William Claiborne, Esquire, on March 13, 1629; "America and West Indies," 1–15, the King's Commission to William Claiborne, "one of the council members and secretary of state for our colony of Virginia, on May 16, 1631.

4. "America and West Indies," 1–15, Captain William Claiborne's case stated against "Lord Baltimore."

5. The *Oxford English Dictionary* defines "pinnace" as a small boat, typically with sails and/or several oars, forming part of the equipment of a warship or other large vessel.

6. Clayton Colman Hall, "Letter of Governor Leonard Calvert to Lord Baltimore, 1638," in *Narratives of Early Maryland, 1633–1684* (New York: Barnes & Noble, 1946), 150–59; John Williams Murray Lee, ed., "Thomas Smith's Account of His Capture, 1635," in *Calvert Papers* (Library of Congress).

7. Hall, "Letter of Governor Leonard Calvert," 147–49; "America and West Indies," 1–15; *Minutes of a County Court Held at St. Maries* (February 12, 1638) (J. Herbert Claiborne, William Claiborne of Kent Island), *The William and Mary Quarterly* 1, no. 2 (1921): 82–84; *Judicial and Testamentary Business of the Provincial Court, 1637–1650* 4: 4, 21–22; "America and West Indies," 1–15, warrant of Cecil Lord Baltimore to Robert Vaughan, commander of Palmer's Island, March 19, 1638; "America and West Indies," 1–15, an Act for the attainder of William Claiborne, gentleman, March 24, 1638.

8. Robert C. Ritchie, *Captain Kidd and the War against the Pirates* (Cambridge, MA: Harvard University Press, 1986), 11.

9. Cotton Mather, "Faithful Warnings to Prevent Fearful Judgments. Uttered in a Brief Discourse, Occasioned, by a Tragical Spectacle, in a Number of Miserables under a Sentence of Death for Piracy," Evans Early American Imprint Collection, www.quod.lib.umich.edu.

10. Colonial governors and officials were not allowed to share in the profits, but they could accept "gifts" and they sometimes openly accepted bribes from those who wanted to secure a privateering commission.

11. Alan Karras, *Smuggling: Contraband and Corruption in World History* (New York: Rowman & Littlefield Publishers, Inc., 2010), 19.

12. Stephen J. Hornsby, *British Atlantic, American Frontier: Spaces of Power in Early Modern British America* (Hanover, NH: University Press of New England, 2005), 97.

13. Allan M. Brandt, *The Cigarette Century: The Rise, Fall and Deadly Persistence of the Product That Defined America* (New York: Basic, 2009), 20–23; Jordan Goodman, *Tobacco in History: The Cultures of Dependence* (London: Routledge, 1993), 158.

14. Hornsby, *British Atlantic, American Frontier*, 88–98.

Part I

15. Edward Ingle, *Captain Richard Ingle: The Maryland "Pirate and Rebel," 1642–1653* (Baltimore: John Murphy & Co., 1884), 30.

16. Ibid., 8–12.

17. Ibid., 10.

18. Ibid., 14.

19. Ibid., 22–24.

20. Ibid., 27–28; Donald Shomette, *Pirates on the Chesapeake: Being a True History of Pirates, Picaroons and Raiders on the Chesapeake Bay, 1610–1807* (Centreville,

MD: Tidewater Publishers, 1985), 31; "Richard Ingle in Maryland," *Maryland Historical Magazine* 1, no. 2 (June 1906): 134.

21. "Thomas Cornwallis against Richard Ingle," in *Proceedings of the Council of Maryland, 1636–1667* (Maryland State Archives) 167, www.aomol.msa. maryland.gov.

22. "The Humble Peticon of Richard Ingle, 24 Feb. 1645," in *Proceedings of the Council of Maryland, 1636–1667* (Maryland State Archives) 165, aomol. msa.maryland.gov.

23. "Richard Ingle in Maryland," 135.

24. Edward Davis has also been listed in the records as Davies, while Lionel Delawafer later changed his name to Wafer as a means of distancing himself from his piratical past.

25. Schomette, *Pirates on the Chesapeake*, 78; "America and West Indies: Value of the goods claimed by (Edward) Davies and his companions, March 28, 1689," in *Calendar of State Papers Colonial, America and West Indies: Volume 13, 1689–1692*, no. 61, edited by J.W. Fortescue (London: Her Majesty's Stationery Office, 1901): 11–20.

26. William Dampier, "Chapter 4," in *A New Voyage Round the World* (London: Argonaut Press, 1927; London: A. and C. Black Ltd., 1937), Project Gutenberg of Australia.

27. Dampier, "Chapters 4–5," in *A New Voyage Round the World*.

28. Shomette, *Pirates on the Chesapeake*, 78; Lionel Delawafer, *A New Voyage and Description of the Isthmus of America*, edited by L.E. Elliott Joyce (Oxford: 1934), xliv.

29. "America and West Indies: February 1692: Affidavit of Captain Simon Rowe, February 12, 1692," in *Calendar of State Papers*, 597–605.

30. "America and West Indies: March 1689: Petition of Micaiah Perry on behalf of Edward Davies and others, March 28, 1689," no. 621.

31. "America and West Indies: November 1690, 17–30: Answer of Lord Howard of Effingham to the petition of Edward Davies and others, November 18, 1690," in *Calendar of State Papers*: no. 1189, 347–67; Shomette, *Pirates on the Chesapeake*, 81.

32. Micaiah has also been spelled Micajah in the records. "America and West Indies: February 1692: Petition of Edward Davies and others, February 18, 1692," no. 2059.

33. William Hand Browne, ed., *Proceedings of the Council of Maryland, 1698–1731*, Vol. 17 (Baltimore: Maryland Historical Society, 1905), 350–51.

34. Ibid.

35. Hind's name has also been spelled Hynd or Hine, and Rhett's name has been spelled as Writt in the records.

36. Shomette, *Pirates on the Chesapeake*, 103–10.

37. John Franklin Jameson, ed., *Privateering and Piracy* (New York: The Macmillan Company, 1923), 253–57.

38. Ritchie, *Captain Kidd*, 2, 28–30.

39. Ibid., 30–32.

40. Ibid., 36–40.

41. Ibid., 54.

42. Jameson, *Privateering and Piracy*, 207–8.

43. Ibid., 208–9, 214.

44. Ibid., 209–11; "America and West Indies: December 1699, 1–15: An account of what Captain Kidd has done abroad, December 4, 1699," in *Calendar of State Papers Colonial, America and West Indies: Volume 17, 1699 and Addenda 1621–1698*, edited by Cecil Headlam (London: His Majesty's Stationery Office, 1908): no. 1034, 564–75.

45. "America and West Indies: October 1699, 26–31: Rear-Admiral Benbow to Mr. Secretary Vernon," *Calendar of State Papers Colonial, America and West Indies, Volume 17, 1699 and Addenda 1621–1698*, no. 907, 500–5.

46. "America and West Indies: June 1699, 21–30," in *Calendar of State Papers Colonial, America and West Indies: Volume 17, 1699 and Addenda 1621–1698*, 291–308.

47. Jameson, *Privateering and Piracy*, 190–257; Shomette, *Pirates on the Chesapeake*, 100–2.

48. Browne, *Proceedings of the Council of Maryland, 1698–1731*, 76–78; Jameson, *Privateering and Piracy*, 200–1; "America and West Indies: June 1699, 12–20: Governor Blakiston to Mr. Secretary Vernon, June 8, 1699," in *Calendar of State Papers Colonial, America and West Indies: Volume 17, 1699 and Addenda 1621–1698*, no. 530i, 283–91.

49. It is entirely plausible, given the year, that Guittar and his men had been privateers operating on behalf of the French, who were at war with the English as part of the Nine Years' War until 1697, when there was a brief truce until the war of Spanish Succession kicked off in 1701.

50. Jameson, *Privateering and Piracy*, 262–72; "A Pirate in the Chesapeake Bay," Maryland Historical Society, www.mdhs.org.

51. Jameson, *Privateering and Piracy*, 268–72; "A Pirate in the Chesapeake Bay."

52. Jameson, *Privateering and Piracy*, 272–75; "America and West Indies: June 1700, 6010: Captain Passenger's Account of the Taking of a French Pirate," in *Calendar of State Papers Colonial, America and West Indies: Volume 18,*

1700, edited by Cecil Headlam (London: His Majesty's Stationery Office, 1910): no. 523ii, 302–29; Ritchie, *Captain Kidd*, 1.

53. Paul also shows up as Paulsgrave or Palgrave in the records.

54. Captain Charles Johnson, *The History of the Pyrates: Volume II*, 201–203, Project Gutenberg.

55. Ibid., 203–4.

56. Ibid., 204–5.

57. "America and West Indies: May 1717, 16–31: Information of Andrew Turbett, Master, and Robert Gilmor, May 31, 1717," in *Calendar of State Papers Colonial, America and West Indies: Volume 29, 1716–1717*, edited by Cecil Headlam (London: His Majesty's Stationery Office, 1930): no. 595i, 303–22.

58. "America and West Indies: May 1717, 16–31: Deposition of John Lucas, May 31, 1717," no. 595ii.

59. Johnson, *The History of the Pyrates: Volume II*, 210–11; "America and West Indies: July 1717, 17–31; Lieutenant Governor Bennett to the Council of Trade and Plantations, July 30, 1717," in *Calendar of State Papers Colonial, America and West Indies: Volume 29, 1716–1717*, no. 677, 344–64.

60. According to South Carolina governor Robert Johnson, all of Worley's men, including Worley himself, perished in the fight. Captain Charles Johnson, *A General History of the Pyrates: Volume I*, 342–46, archive.org; "America and West Indies: December 1718, 11–19: Governor and Council of South Carolina to the Council of Trade and Plantations, December 12, 1719," in *Calendar of State Papers Colonial, America and West Indies: Volume 30, 1717–1718*, no. 787, 404–24.

61. Shomette, *Pirates on the Chesapeake*, 192.

62. "America and West Indies: June 1718: Governor Johnson to the Council of Trade and Plantations, June 18, 1718," in *Calendar of State Papers Colonial, America and West Indies: Volume 30, 1717–1718*, no. 556, 264–87.

63. "America and West Indies: February 1720, 1–8: Petition of the Council and Assembly of the Settlements in South Carolina to the King, February 3, 1720," in *Calendar of State Papers Colonial, America and West Indies: Volume 31, 1719–1720*, edited by Cecil Headlam (London: His Majesty's Stationery Office, 1933): no. 541, 323–52.

64. "America and West Indies: August 1718: Lt. Governor Spotswood to the Council of Trade and Plantations, August 14, 1717," in *Calendar of State Papers Colonial, America and West Indies: Volume 30, 1717–1718*, no. 657, 327–43.

65. "America and West Indies: December 1718, 22–31: Lt. Governor Spotswood to the Council of Trade and Plantations, December 22,

1718," in *Calendar of State Papers Colonial, America and West Indies: Volume 30, 1717–1718*, no. 800, 424–46.

66. "America and West Indies: December 1718, 22–31: Lieutenant Governor Spotswood to the Council of Trade and Plantations, December 22, 1718"; Johnson, *A General History of the Pyrates: Volume I*, 82–85.

Part II

67. Shomette, *Pirates on the Chesapeake*, 260.

68. The entire list of known letters for Maryland can be found in Bernard C. Steiner's "Maryland Privateers in the American Revolution," *Maryland Historical Magazine* 3, no. 2 (1908): 101–3. The printed abstracts of the letters contain the date on which the letters were issued, the name of the vessel and its character (as ship, brig, sloop, et cetera) the number of guns and crewmembers, the amount of bond given (which was always $5,000 or some multiple of that sum and which never surpassed $20,000), the names of the officers and of the two bonders (one of whom was always the master of the vessel) and the names of the owners and of a witness (who was frequently Thomas Johnson Jr.).

69. Shannon Byrne, "Baltimore's Piratical Patriot Privateers" (Seminar Paper, University of Maryland Francis King Carey School of Law, 2015), 4.

70. William Hand Browne, ed., *Archives of Maryland: Journal and Correspondence of the Maryland Council of Safety, July 7–December 31, 1776*, Vol. 12 (Baltimore: Maryland Historical Society, 1893), 274; William James Morgan, ed., "Application for Commission of Letter of Marque and Reprisal for the Maryland Sloop *Baltimore Hero*," in *Naval Documents of the American Revolution*, Vol. 6 (Washington, D.C.: 1970), 864.

71. William James Morgan, ed., "Governor Craister Greathead to Governor Johannes de Graaff" and "Deposition of Foster McConnell," in *Naval Documents of the American Revolution*, Vol. 7 (Washington, D.C.: 1972), 507–9, 917–19.

72. William Hand Browne, ed., *Archives of Maryland: Journal and Correspondence of the Maryland Council of Safety, April 1, 1778–October 26, 1779*, Vol. 21 (Baltimore: Maryland Historical Society, 1901), 393–94.

73. *The Pennsylvania Packet or the General Advertiser* (Philadelphia), Tuesday, June 22, 1779, datelined Annapolis, June 18, pg. 2; Browne, ed., *Archives of Maryland: Journal and Correspondence of the Maryland Council of*

Safety, April 1, 1778–October 26, 1779, Vol. 21, 453; *New Jersey Gazette* (Burlington), November 10, 1779, datelined Philadelphia, November 2, pg. 2.

74. Isaac J. Greenwood Jr., "Cruizing on the Chesapeake in 1781," *Maryland Historical Magazine* 5, no. 2 (1910): 123–25.

75. Wheland also appears in the records as Whalen, Wheeland or Walen.

76. Greenwood, "Cruizing on the Chesapeake in 1781," 126.

77. Ibid., 127–28.

78. Ibid., 128–29.

79. Ibid., 129–30.

80. Quoted in Shomette, *Pirates in the Chesapeake*, 256.

81. William James Morgan, ed., "Deposition of Mores Yell, July 27th, 1776," in *Naval Documents of the American Revolution*, Vol. 5 (Washington, D.C.: 1970), 1247–48.

82. Ibid., 1248.

83. Ibid.

84. Fallin is also in the records as Fallen.

85. Morgan, "Brigadier General Henry Hooper to Daniel of St. Thomas Jenifer," 1296.

86. *Calendar of Maryland State Papers: Executive Miscellaneous*, Vol. 5 (Annapolis, MD: Hall of Records Commission, 1958), 57–58.

87. Shomette, *Pirates on the Chesapeake*, 260.

88. *Calendar of Maryland State Papers: The Red Books*, Vol. 4, no. 3 (Annapolis, MD: Hall of Records Commission, 1955), 63.

89. Shomette, *Pirates on the Chesapeake*, 261–63.

90. *Calendar of Maryland State Papers: The Red Books*, Vol. 4, no. 3, 119.

91. Quoted in Shomette, *Pirates on the Chesapeake*, 272–73.

92. Whaley is also in the records as Walley.

93. "Action Between American and British Barges in the Chesapeake Bay, November 1782," in *Maryland Historical Magazine* 4, no. 2 (1909): 115–16.

94. Ibid.

95. Ibid., 117.

96. Ibid.

97. Ibid., 118, 120.

98. Ibid. 118–20, 125; Shomette, *Pirates on the Chesapeake*, 297.

99. "Action Between American and British Barges," 124.

Part III

100. Peter Andreas, *Smuggler Nation: How Illicit Trade Made America* (New York: Oxford University Press, 2013), 63.
101. Ibid., 64–68.
102. Ibid., 68–70.
103. James Madison, "June 19, 1812: Proclamation of a State of War with Great Britain," University of Virginia, Miller Center, www.millercenter.org.
104. Andreas, *Smuggler Nation*, 80–83.
105. Scott S. Sheads, "Privateers," Maryland in the War of 1812: Celebrating the 200th Anniversary of the War of 1812, www.maryland1812.com.
106. Cindy Vallar, "Fell's Point and the Baltimore Privateers," Pirates and Privateers: The History of Maritime Piracy, www.cindyvallar.com.
107. Toni Ahrens, *Design Makes a Difference: Shipbuilding in Baltimore 1795–1835* (n.p.: Heritage Books, 1998), 104.
108. Jerome R. Garitee, *The Republic's Private Navy: The American Privateering Business as Practiced by Baltimore during the War of 1812* (Middletown, CT: Wesleyan University, 1977); Vallar, "Fell's Point and the Baltimore Privateers."
109. The United States Navy recognized his importance by naming a World War II destroyer for him. Frank White Jr., ed., "The *Comet* Harasses the British," *Maryland Historical Magazine* 53, no. 4 (December 1958): 295–99.
110. Ibid., 298–301.
111. Ibid., 298, 303–5.
112. Vallar, "Fell's Point and the Baltimore Privateers"; Ralph D. Paine, "The Brilliant Era of 1812," in *The Old Merchant Marine* (1919), eBook.
113. Quoted in Edgar Stanton Maclay, *A History of American Privateers* (New York: D. Appleton and Co., 1899), 279–300.
114. Quoted in Paine, "The Brilliant Era of 1812."
115. Garitee, *The Republic's Private Navy*, 159–60.
116. Ibid., 161.
117. Quoted in Vallar, "Fell's Point and the Baltimore Privateers."
118. Ibid.
119. Quoted in Sheads, "Privateers."
120. Ibid.
121. John Philips Cranwell and William Bowers Crane, *Men of Marque: A History of the Private Armed Vessels Out of Baltimore During the War of 1812* (New York: W.W. Norton & Co., 1940), 13.
122. "Another Old Defenders Gone," *Baltimore Sun*, January 16, 1861.

123. Charles Ball even wrote a memoir of his experiences in *A Narrative of the Life and Adventures of Charles Ball*. Sheads, "Privateers."
124. George Little, *Life on the Ocean; or Twenty Years at Sea: Being the Personal Adventures of the Author*, second edition (Boston: Waite, Pierce and Company, 1844), chapter XVII, 194–99, eBook.
125. Ibid.
126. Ibid.
127. Ibid.
128. Ibid.
129. Ibid., 200–9.
130. Ibid.
131. Ibid.
132. Ibid., 210–20.
133. Ibid.
134. Ibid.
135. *Vermont Gazette* (Bennington), August 31, 1812, 3, Newspapers.com.
136. Donald Shomette, *Shipwrecks on the Chesapeake* (Centreville, MD: Tidewater Publishers, 1982), 87–93.
137. Ibid.
138. Ibid.
139. "Joshua Barney," American Battlefield Trust, www.battlefields.org.

Part IV

140. Donald Barr Chidsey, *The American Privateers* (New York: Dodd, Mead and Company, 1962), 147–48.
141. Eric Mills, *Chesapeake Bay in the Civil War* (Centreville, MD: Tidewater Publishers, 1996), 3–4.
142. Ibid., 12.
143. Ibid., 17.
144. Quoted in Mills, *Chesapeake Bay in the Civil War*, 208.
145. *Official Records of the Union and Confederate Navies in the War of Rebellion*, Series 1, Volume 5 (Washington, D.C.: Government Printing Office, 1897), 323–24.
146. Ibid., 327–28; Mills, *Chesapeake Bay in the Civil War*, 212–14.
147. John Yates Beall, *Memoir of John Yates Beall: His Life, Trial, Correspondence, Diary, and Private Manuscript Found among His Papers* (Montreal, CAN: Printed by John Lovell, 1865), 19–20.

148. Ibid., 23–24.

149. Ibid., 24; William Washington Baker, *Memoirs of Service with John Yates Beall*, edited by D.S. Freeman (Richmond, VA: Richmond Press, 1910), 18.

150. Some sources say the second-in-command was Roy McDonald, while others say it was Bennet Graham Burley.

151. Baker, *Memoirs of Service with John Yates Beall*, 17–18.

152. Ibid., 19.

153. Ibid., 19–24.

154. Ibid., 26–28.

155. Ibid., 29–30.

156. Ibid., 30–33.

157. John W. Headley, *Confederate Operations in Canada and New York* (n.p.: Neale Publishing Co., 1906, reprint ed., Time-Life Books Inc., 1981), 251–53; Beall, *Memoir of John Yates Beall*, 61.

158. *Iolus* also appears in the records as *Eolus*.

159. *The War of the Rebellion: A Compilation of the Official Records of the Union and Confederate Armies*, Series I, Volume 33 (Washington, D.C.: Government Printing Office, 1891), 232.

160. Mills, *Chesapeake Bay in the Civil War*, 266.

161. Quoted in Mills, *Chesapeake Bay in the Civil War*, 266.

162. *The War of the Rebellion: A Compilation of the Official Records of the Union and Confederate Armies*, Series I, Volume 46 (Washington, D.C.: Government Printing Office, 1894), 1306.

163. Ibid.

164. Ibid., 1306–7.

165. Ibid., 1307.

166. Earl J. Hess, *Civil War Logistics: A Study of Military Transportation* (Baton Rouge: Louisiana State University Press, 2017), Chapter 10, eBook.

Part V

167. It was also referred to as the Maryland Fishery Force.

168. Quoted in John R. Wennersten, *The Oyster Wars of the Chesapeake Bay*, second edition (Washington, D.C.: Eastern Branch Press, 2007), 11.

169. Ibid.; Zoe Friedman, "The Oyster Wars of Chesapeake Bay: How Regulatory Compromise Created Conflict," *International Journal of Naval History*, November 2, 2018, www.ijnhonline.org.

170. Wennersten, *The Oyster Wars of the Chesapeake Bay*, 11; "Oyster Wars," *Baltimore Sun*, February 10, 2015, www.baltimoresun.com.

171. Wennersten, *The Oyster Wars of the Chesapeake Bay*, 13–14.

172. Ibid., 14–17, 27; Anna Maria Gillis, "Oyster Wars: Wayward Watermen of the Chesapeake Bay," *Humanities* 32, no. 3 (May/June 2011), www.neh.gov; James Tice Moore, "Gunfire on the Chesapeake: Governor Cameron and the Oyster Pirates, 1882–1885," *The Virginia Magazine of History and Biography* 90, no. 3 (July 1982): 367.

173. Ross M. Kimmel, "Oyster Wars: The Historic Fight for the Bay's Riches," Maryland Department of Natural Resources, www.fliphtml5.com.

174. Moore, "Gunfire on the Chesapeake," 367–68.

175. "Oyster Wars of the Lower Chesapeake Bay: The War of 1882," The Mariners' Museum, www.marinersmuseum.org; Moore, "Gunfire on the Chesapeake," 367.

176. "Oyster Wars of the Lower Chesapeake Bay: The War of 1882"; Moore, "Gunfire on the Chesapeake," 369–70.

177. Moore, "Gunfire on the Chesapeake," 370–71.

178. Ibid., 371–72.

179. Ibid., 372; "Oyster Wars of the Lower Chesapeake Bay: The Second Oyster War."

180. Moore, "Gunfire on the Chesapeake," 373; "Oyster Wars of the Lower Chesapeake Bay: The Second Oyster War."

181. Moore, "Gunfire on the Chesapeake," 373; "Oyster Wars of the Lower Chesapeake Bay: The Pirate Brides," *The Virginia Magazine of History and Biography* 90, no. 3 (July 1982).

182. Moore, "Gunfire on the Chesapeake," 373.

183. Ibid., 375–76.

184. "Piratical Oyster Crews: The Desperadoes Very Free in the Use of Their Fire-Arms; The Police Boat and a Magistrate's Residence Showered with Bullets—Bloody Deeds Anticipated," *New York Times*, February 15, 1884, www.dnr.maryland.gov.

185. Ibid.

186. Ibid.

187. Ibid.

188. Wennersten, *The Oyster Wars of the Chesapeake Bay*, 88–89.

189. Kimmel, "Oyster Wars: The Historic Fight for the Bay's Riches."

190. "An Oyster Pirate Killed: Captain Whitehouse Found Dredging and Shot Dead in a Fight," *New York Times*, February 20, 1888, www.dnr.maryland.gov.

191. Ibid.

192. Ibid.

193. Ibid.

194. Wennersten, *The Oyster Wars of the Chesapeake Bay*, 76–77.

195. Ibid., 77–78.

196. Ibid., 78.

197. Ibid., 78–79.

198. Ibid., 73; "Captain T.C.B. Howard of the Steamer *McLane* of the Maryland Fishery Force Gives the Following Story of the Battle with the Oyster Pirates," *New York Times*, December 13, 1888, www.dnr.maryland.gov.

199. Ibid.

200. Ibid.

201. Ibid.

202. Ibid.; Wennersten, *The Oyster Wars of the Chesapeake Bay*, 80–82.

203. "Captain T.C.B. Howard of the Steamer *McLane*."

204. Wennersten, *The Oyster Wars of the Chesapeake Bay*, 89–90.

205. Ibid., 96–97.

206. Ibid., 102–5.

207. Ibid., 123–24.

208. Ibid., 124–25; Friedman, "The Oyster Wars of Chesapeake Bay."

BIBLIOGRAPHY

Books

Ahrens, Toni. *Design Makes a Difference: Shipbuilding in Baltimore 1795–1835.* Berwyn Heights, MD: Heritage Books, 1998.

Andreas, Peter. *Smuggler Nation: How Illicit Trade Made America.* New York: Oxford University Press, 2013.

Brandt, Allan M. *The Cigarette Century: The Rise, Fall and Deadly Persistence of the Product That Defined America.* New York: Basic, 2009.

Brenner, Robert. *Merchants and Revolution: Commercial Change, Political Conflict and London's Overseas Traders.* London: Verso, 2003.

Chidsey, Donald Barr. *The American Privateers.* New York: Dodd, Mead & Company, 1962.

Cranwell, John Philips, and William Bowers Crane. *Men of Marque: A History of the Private Armed Vessels Out of Baltimore During the War of 1812.* New York: W.W. Norton & Co., 1940.

Eller, Ernest McNeil, ed. *Chesapeake Bay in the American Revolution.* Centreville, MD: Tidewater Publishers, 1981.

Garitee, Jerome R. *The Republic's Private Navy: The American Privateering Business as Practiced by Baltimore during the War of 1812.* Middletown, CT: Wesleyan University, 1977.

Goodman, Jordan. *Tobacco in History: The Cultures of Dependence.* London: Routledge, 1993.

Headley, John W. *Confederate Operations in Canada and New York*. New York: Time-Life Books Inc., 1981. First published 1906 by Neale Publishing Co.

Hornsby, Stephen J. *British Atlantic, American Frontier: Spaces of Power in Early Modern British America*. Lebanon, NH: University Press of New England, 2005.

Ingle, Edward. *Captain Richard Ingle, the Maryland "Pirate and Rebel," 1642–1653*. Baltimore: John Murphy & Co., 1884.

Johnson, Captain Charles. *A General History of the Pyrates*. Vol. I. London: Ch. Rivington, J. Lacy and J. Stone, 1724. Archive.org.

———. *A General History of the Pyrates*. Vol. II. London: Ch. Rivington, J. Lacy and J. Stone, 1724. Project Gutenburg.

Karras, Alan. *Smuggling: Contraband and Corruption in World History*. New York: Rowman & Littlefield Publishers Inc., 2010.

Mills, Eric. *Chesapeake Bay in the Civil War*. Centreville, MD: Tidewater Publishers, 1996.

Ritchie, Robert C. *Captain Kidd and the War against the Pirates*. Cambridge, MA: Harvard University Press, 1986.

Sheads, Scott, and Jerome Bird. *Privateers from the Chesapeake: The Story of Chasseur, the "Pride of Baltimore," and the War of 1812*. Baltimore: Pride of Baltimore, 2001.

Shomette, Donald. *Pirates on the Chesapeake: Being a True History of Pirates, Picaroons, and Raiders on the Chesapeake Bay, 1610–1807*. Centreville, MD: Tidewater Publishers, 1985.

———. *Shipwrecks on the Chesapeake*. Centreville, MD: Tidewater Publishers, 1982.

Szaltis, Leonard. *Chesapeake Bay Privateers in the Revolution*. Charleston, SC: The History Press, 2019.

Journals

Friedman, Zoe. "The Oyster Wars of Chesapeake Bay: How Regulatory Compromise Created Conflict." *International Journal of Naval History* (November 2, 2018), www.ijnhonline.org.

Gillis, Anna Maria. "Oyster Wars: Wayward Watermen of the Chesapeake Bay." *Humanities* 32, no. 3 (May/June 2011), www.neh.gov.

Moore, James Tice. "Gunfire on the Chesapeake: Governor Cameron and the Oyster Pirates, 1882–1885." *The Virginia Magazine of History and Biography* 90, no. 3 (July 1982): 367–77.

"Richard Ingle in Maryland." *Maryland Historical Magazine* 1, no. 2 (June 1906): 125–40.

Steiner, Bernard C. "Maryland Privateers in the American Revolution." *Maryland Historical Magazine* 3, no. 2 (June 1908): 99–103.

Other Publications

Byrne, Shannon. "Baltimore's Piratical Patriot Privateers." Seminar paper, University of Maryland Francis King Carey School of Law, 2015.

Newspapers

Baltimore Sun. "Another Old Defender Gone." January 16, 1861. www.newspapers.com.

———. "Oyster Wars." February 10, 2015. www.baltimoresun.com.

New York Times. "Capt. T.C.B. Howard of the Steamer *McLane* of the Maryland Fishery Force Gives the Following Story of the Battle with the Oyster Pirates." December 13, 1888. www.dnr.maryland.gov.

———. "An Oyster Pirate Killed: Capt. Whitehouse Found Dredging and Shot Dead in a Fight." February 20, 1888. www.dnr.maryland.gov.

———. "Piratical Oyster Crews: The Desperadoes Very Free in the Use of Their Fire-Arms; The Police Boat and a Magistrate's Residence Showered with Bullets—Bloody Deeds Anticipated." February 15, 1884. www.dnr.maryland.gov.

Pennsylvania Packet or General Advertiser, June 22, 1779. www.newspapers.com.

Published Primary Sources

"Action Between American and British Barges in the Chesapeake Bay, November 1782." *Maryland Historical Magazine* 4, no. 2 (1909): 115–33.

Baker, William Washington. *Memoirs of Service with John Yates Beall.* Edited by D.S. Freeman. Richmond, VA: Richmond Press, 1910.

Beall, John Yates. *Memoir of John Yates Beall: His Life, Trial, Correspondence, Diary and Private Manuscript Found Among His Papers.* Montreal, CAN: John Lovell, 1865.

Browne, William Hand, ed. *Archives of Maryland: Journal and Correspondence of the Maryland Council of Safety, July 7–December 31, 1776.* Vol. 12. Baltimore: Maryland Historical Society, 1893.

———. *Archives of Maryland: Journal and Correspondence of the Maryland Council of Safety, April 1, 1778–October 26, 1779.* Vol. 21. Baltimore: Maryland Historical Society, 1901.

———. *Proceedings of the Council of Maryland, 1636–1667.* Vol. 3. Maryland State Archives, 1885.

———. *Proceedings of the Council of Maryland, 1681–1685/6.* Vol. 17. Baltimore: Maryland Historical Society, 1898.

———. *Proceedings of the Council of Maryland, 1698–1731.* Vol. 17. Baltimore: Maryland Historical Society, 1905.

Calendar of Maryland State Papers: Executive Miscellaneous. Vol. 5. Annapolis, MD: Hall of Records Commission, 1958.

Calendar of Maryland State Papers: The Red Books. Vol. 4, no. 3. Annapolis, MD: Hall of Records Commission, 1955.

Dampier, William. *A New Voyage Round the World.* London: Adam and Charles Black, 1697. Project Gutenberg of Australia.

Delawafer, Lionel. *A New Voyage and Description of the Isthmus of America.* Edited by L.E. Elliott Joyce. Oxford: Ashgate Publishing, 1934.

Greenwood, John, Jr., and Isaac J. Greenwood. "Cruizing on the Chesapeake in 1781." *Maryland Historical Magazine* 5, no. 2 (1910): 123–31.

Hall, Clayton Colman. *Narratives of Early Maryland, 1633–1684.* New York: Barnes & Noble Publishers, 1946. Internet Archive.

Hess, Earl J. *Civil War Logistics: A Study of Military Transportation.* Baton Rouge: Louisiana State University Press, 2017.

Jameson, John Franklin. *Privateering and Piracy in the Colonial Period: Illustrative Documents.* New York: Macmillan Company, 1923.

Lee, John Williams Murray, ed. "Thomas Smith's Account of His Capture, 1635." *Calvert Papers.* Library of Congress.

Little, George. *Life on the Ocean; or Twenty Years at Sea: Being the Personal Adventures of the Author.* 2nd edition. Boston: Waite, Pierce and Company, 1844.

Mather, Cotton. "Faithful Warnings to Prevent Fearful Judgments. Uttered in a Brief Discourse, Occasioned, by a Tragical Spectacle, in a Number of Miserables under a Sentence of Death for Piracy." *Evans Early American Imprint Collection.* www.quod.lib.umich.edu.

Morgan, William James, ed. *Naval Documents of the American Revolution.* Vol. 5. Washington, D.C.: Naval History Division, 1970.

———. *Naval Documents of the American Revolution.* Vol. 6. Washington, D.C.: Naval History Division, 1972.

———. *Naval Documents of the American Revolution.* Vol. 7. Washington, D.C.: Naval History Division, 1976.

———. *Naval Documents of the American Revolution.* Vol. 8. Washington, D.C.: Naval History Division, 1980.

Murphy, D.F. *The Jeff Davis Piracy Cases: Full Report of the Trial of William Smith for Piracy, As One of the Crew of the Confederate Privateer, the* Jeff Davis*: Before Judges Grier and Cadwalader, in the Circuit Court of the United States, for the Eastern District of Pennsylvania, Held at Philadelphia, in October 1861.* Philadelphia: King & Baird Printers, 1861.

Official Records of the Union and Confederate Navies in the War of Rebellion. Series 1, Vol. 5. Washington, D.C.: Government Printing Office, 1897.

Pleasants, J. Hall. *Journal and Correspondence of the Council of Maryland, 1781–1784.* Vol. 48. Annapolis: Maryland State Archives, 1784.

Sainsbury, W. Noel, and J.W. Fortescue. *Calendar of State Papers Colonial, America and West Indies.* Vol. 10, *1677–1680.* London: Her Majesty's Stationery Office, 1896. www.british-history.ac.uk.

The War of the Rebellion: A Compilation of the Official Records of the Union and Confederate Armies. Series I, Vol. 33. Washington, D.C.: Government Printing Office, 1891.

The War of the Rebellion: A Compilation of the Official Records of the Union and Confederate Armies. Series I, Vol. 46. Washington, D.C.: Government Printing Office, 1894.

White, Frank, Jr., ed. "The *Comet* Harasses the British." *Maryland Historical Magazine* 53, no. 4 (December 1958): 295–316.

Web Sources

American Battlefield Trust. "Joshua Barney." www.battlefields.org.

Bailey, Roger A. "Confederate Privateers and Cruisers in the Civil War." American Battlefield Trust. www.battlefields.org.

Kimmel, Ross M. "Oyster Wars: The Historic Fight for the Bay's Riches." Maryland Department of Natural Resources. www.fliphtml5.com.

Madison, James. "June 19, 1812: Proclamation of a State of War with Great Britain." University of Virginia, Miller Center. www.millercenter.org.

Mariners' Museum. "Oyster Wars of the Lower Chesapeake Bay." www.marinersmuseum.org.

Maryland Historical Society. "A Pirate in the Chesapeake Bay." www.mdhs.org.

Sheads, Scott S. "Privateers." Maryland in the War of 1812: Celebrating the 200th Anniversary of the War of 1812. www.maryland1812.com.

Vallar, Cindy. "Fell's Point and the Baltimore Privateers." Pirates and Privateers: The History of Maritime Piracy. www.cindyvallar.com.

Virginia Places. "The Chesapeake Bay: Avenue for Attack." www.virginiaplaces.org.

INDEX

V

Victoria J. Peed 116, 118, 119

W

Watt's Creek 32
Wentworth, Caesar 83
Whaley, Zedekiah 68, 69, 70, 71, 143
Wheland, Joseph 60, 61, 62, 63,
　　64, 65, 66, 67, 68, 143
Whidah Galley 47
Whitehouse, William Frank 123, 124
Wilson, Charles 54
Wood, John Taylor 97, 99, 100, 106
Worley, Richard 47, 48, 49, 141

Y

Yankes, Captain 29
Yell, Mores 64, 65, 143